PRAISE FOR

Do It Anyway

"Tasha Cobbs Leonard's voice has resonated across the globe through her music, but now she offers us a profound glimpse into her intellectual and spiritual depth. This book transcends mere melody to reveal Tasha as a profound thinker and an inspirational leader. Prepare to be invigorated to claim every promise, realize every dream, cast aside every excuse, and embrace every God-given desire within your heart."

—TRAVIS AND JACKIE GREENE,
pastors of Forward City Church

"People would never believe that Tasha Cobbs Leonard's royal, powerful presence was borne out of a modest, vulnerable place. As her friend, I have a hard time believing anything could ever shake her. But this book is full of those tough, unsafe, less-than-gospel-legend moments that produced a jewel of a woman and leader. *Do It Anyway* is a must-read."

—JONATHAN MCREYNOLDS,
Grammy Award–winning gospel artist

"Tasha Cobbs Leonard's story gives endless hope and inspiration. *Do It Anyway* is a phrase that every believer should live by because we walk by faith and not by sight!"

—CECE WINANS,
Grammy Award–winner and author of *Believe for It*

"Tasha Cobbs Leonard has done it again! It's usually in the songs she writes, but now it's in the book she wrote. We read about God-sent revelation along with real-life experiences. It convinces us that living 'the life' is possible, even with detours." —KIERRA SHEARD-KELLY, author and Grammy-nominated artist

"*Do It Anyway* is a must-read if you want to experience the amazing life ahead that is right at your fingertips . . . conquering fear, doubt, and everyday life circumstances that simply have gotten the best of us." —ONIKA TANYA MARAJ, aka Nicki Minaj

"*Do It Anyway* is an inspiring collection of stories from my hero Tasha Cobbs Leonard. These stories challenge me and put a demand on my faith and my understanding of who God is. Each story is brilliantly told." —NAOMI RAINE, Grammy Award–winning Christian artist

"This riveting work by Tasha Cobbs Leonard is more than a book; it's a blueprint to God's best. She highlights the truth that the conditions will never be perfect for you to progress. Some books tell you that you need to get over certain challenges like grief, fear, and disappointment; Tasha shows you how. If you are ready to stay the same, don't read this book. Never mind; read it anyway!" —DHARIUS DANIELS, senior pastor of Change Church and author of *Relational Intelligence*

DO IT
ANYWAY

DO IT ANYWAY

Don't Give Up Before It Gets Good

Tasha Cobbs Leonard

with Travis Thrasher

Foreword by Sarah Jakes Roberts

WATERBROOK

Details in some anecdotes and stories have been changed to protect the identities of the persons involved.

Published in the United States by WaterBrook, an imprint of Random House, a division WATERBROOK and colophon are registered trademarks of Penguin Random House LLC.

Grateful acknowledgment is made to Capitol Christian Music Group Publishing for permission to reprint excerpts from "Never Gave Up" written by Tasha Cobbs Leonard and Kenneth Leonard, Jr., copyright © 2020 by Tasha Cobbs Music Group/Meadowgreen Music Company (ASCAP)/Capitol CMG Paragon/KMLJ Productions (BMI) (Admin at CapitolCMGPublishing.com) and "Gotta Believe" written by Tasha Cobbs Leonard, copyright © 2021 by Tasha Cobbs Music Group/Meadowgreen Music Company (ASCAP) (Admin. at CapitolCMGPublishing.com). Reprinted by permission.

Library of Congress Cataloging-in-Publication Data
Names: Cobbs-Leonard, Tasha, author.
Title: Do it anyway: don't give up before it gets good /
Tasha Cobbs Leonard; with Travis Thrasher.
Description: First edition. | Colorado Springs: WaterBrook, [2024] |
Includes bibliographical references.
Identifiers: LCCN 2023046527 | ISBN 9780593600870 (hardcover) |
ISBN 9780593600894 (ebook)
Subjects: LCSH: Perseverance (Ethics)—Religious aspects—Christianity. |
Faith—Religious aspects—Christianity.
Classification: LCC BV4598.3 .C633 2024 | DDC 241/.4—dc23/eng/20231214
LC record available at https://lccn.loc.gov/2023046527

Printed in the United States of America on acid-free paper

waterbrookmultnomah.com

2 4 6 8 9 7 5 3 1

First Edition

Book design by Fritz Metsch

Most WaterBrook books are available at special quantity discounts for bulk purchase for premiums, fundraising, and corporate and educational needs by organizations, churches, and businesses. Special books or book excerpts also can be created to fit specific needs. For details, contact specialmarketscms@penguinrandomhouse.com.

To my father, Bishop Fritz Cobbs,
for the invaluable lesson you've taught me
to stay at the feet of Jesus.

FOREWORD

When I was growing up in church, Resurrection Sunday was the one Sunday of the year we could count on the church being jam-packed. Everyone from regular church attendees to those who make their annual appearance files through the doors to celebrate that Jesus rose from the grave. Everyone came dressed in their Sunday best to marvel at speeches, sermons, and productions that praise the hallmark of our faith. Less packed were the Good Friday services, where we gathered to acknowledge the pain and suffering that was paid for our salvation.

It's not unique to Christians to give more attention to moments of victory than those of suffering. All of humanity knows a thing or two about burying pain with smiles, performance, and servitude. A person is rarely willing to break open their soul for the world to see the pain behind the gain, but when they do, it makes us all feel less alone. I wasn't sure I could ever experience that in spaces of faith. Too often, we are lauded for our ability to hide our truth and pretend we're fine when we're in pain, but I didn't experience that with Tasha.

Like many of you, I was looking on from the outside as her anointing ascended to unprecedented heights. It was undeniable that she'd been called to bridge the gaps that kept communities of faith divided. A multicultural grace that translated regardless of denomination or race is too unusual to ignore. There was no doubt that God was giving her the wind to take the world by storm.

So many in her position would have allowed the impact to speak on their behalf, but not Tasha. Whenever our paths crossed, she dared to give voice to the storm. She told me once that she never wanted to be guilty of taking glory that she knew belonged to God. Tasha shared with me the anointing and the scars. She allowed me to see that the oil that moved a room came from her wounds.

I thought she was being a good friend to another woman in ministry, but then I attended an event she hosted for creatives in ministry. I learned that she is not just a good friend; she's a leader on a mission to empower every person she encounters to accomplish their destiny anyway. With each turn of a page, you will realize that this is not just Tasha's story, but it's yours and mine too.

If she could step in the ring and fight your battle for you, she would suit up without thinking twice—I know her heart. But this confrontation is for your destiny, and you are the only one who can render it impotent. So she's done the next best thing. Tasha has done the work of retracing her steps so that you can be led forward with the same level of faith and determination that helped Jesus complete His assignment. You'll find this book as a companion for every season and stage of your life, and though I may be a little biased, I have to say that you truly could not have a more experienced or compassionate coach in your corner.

—Sarah Jakes Roberts, bestselling author of *Woman Evolve*

CONTENTS

PROLOGUE

There are moments in life when we have to live out the message we say we believe, and those moments usually come when we least expect them. For years, I had been preaching and singing that God is the God of peace, that He's the God who silences the chaos in our lives. But at the start of 2014, after a record-setting "Break Every Chain" year, I found myself suffering through the worst pain I had ever experienced in my life. And I had to do it as the world watched.

On January 18, 2014, I arrived at the Stellar Gospel Music Awards with joy and disbelief. I was still digesting how I had gotten there—and why me? I had seven Stellar nominations and the opportunity to lead worship from the Stellar stage! This was gospel music's biggest night, and for the first time, I wasn't watching from my living room couch. I was a living, breathing, and singing example of Ephesians 3:20:

> God can do anything, you know—far more than you could ever imagine or guess or request in your wildest dreams! He does it not by pushing us around but by working within us, his Spirit deeply and gently within us.

I was riding an unbelievable wave that had started almost a year before when *Grace*, my first album with a label, released. It made the top-ten list of *Billboard*'s Top Gospel Albums and remained there all year. "Break Every Chain" was on this album, and it was now played and sung all over the world. The week after the Stellars, I was heading to the Grammys, where I had two nominations.

Oh my goodness, everything is moving so fast, I thought. *This* has *to be God.*

When they announced the New Artist of the Year and called my name, it was extra special because my dad was there! When he told me earlier that week that he was coming with my mom to the awards show, I was speechless. *Daddy's gonna actually miss a church service?*

Bishop Fritz Cobbs had been a pastor since I was ten years old. We all understood the assignment our family had to Jesup New Life Ministries and the Wayne County community, so I never pressed him to miss a Sunday morning service. I could probably count on one hand how many Daddy had missed in his life. Even our vacations would be scheduled around Sundays. But he put that aside to be with me on this night.

As I took the stage, I could truly sense God in the room. I'm always so grateful for His presence. What a privilege and an honor! Every time I stand to minister, my desire is always God's presence. We're nothing without *Him*! As I sang "Break Every Chain" under the spotlight, I could feel His strength resting on me.

After I picked up three awards, including New Artist of the Year, a group of us called an impromptu celebration in the suite of William Murphy, my pastor and mentor at the time. I called my father, saying, "Hey, Daddy. We're hanging out in Pastor Murphy's room. If y'all want to come up, let me know." It was nearly one in the morning, so the chance of my parents joining us was very low (actually nonexistent).

"We'll be there in a few minutes," he responded.

He said yes?

Once again, I couldn't believe it! My parents weren't the hang-out types, so this was another big deal. This special time with them meant more to me than any award or applause. On this night of celebration, they ventured out and we had a ball! My dad was a man of few words, but when something witty came to him, I'd put him up against any comedian. He was hilarious. If preaching didn't work out, he could easily fall back on stand-up. I was expecting security to knock on the door any second to ask us to keep down the noise because Daddy had us screaming with laughter until three in the morning, talking about everything. Pastor Murphy was rolling on the floor in tears.

When I finally walked my parents toward the elevator, they were both beaming with pride from witnessing all that God was doing. I snapped a photo of my father standing at the elevator, holding one of my Stellar Awards in his hand and grinning with youthful glee. That trophy was my gift of thanks to them for the many sacrifices they made so that my brother and I would want for nothing. Daddy had built a special curio cabinet to house and display my awards.

Just before he stepped into the elevator, this man of very few words said something he always told me: "Daddy loves you, baby." He gave me a kiss on my cheek, and then the elevator doors closed. My parents were leaving the next morning.

That was the last time I would ever see and speak to my father. None of us could have imagined that God would call him to his eternal home the following day.

Over the years, Daddy had given me invaluable gifts: a rich faith in Jesus, a strong work ethic, a heart for ministry, and many more, including the mentality and grit to live out the message we Christians say we believe, especially when we don't want to. The moments when all that seems left to do is surrender to our circumstances are precisely the moments when we must press on and do the hard thing. To follow God when the way seems impossible, persevere in faith even when the odds are stacked—this is what it means to "do it anyway."

I've had years of thinking on this principle and putting it into practice, and I know for certain now that my dad was right—because on the other side of endurance is breakthrough and transformation. This one lesson has changed my life in amazing ways time and time again. And I think it will do the same for you.

DO IT
ANYWAY

1

IN LIFE-CHANGING MOMENTS

"Tasha, you gotta sing," the choir told me. I stood in the fellowship hall of Bennett Union Baptist Church in my hometown of Jesup, Georgia, surrounded by a room full of teenagers looking at me to be the remedy to our problem. Preston, our lead singer, had gotten in a car wreck. He was fine but wasn't going to make it to our performance. We needed someone to take the lead.

We were part of a community choir, Sounds of Harmony, formed by a group of us teenagers just a few weeks prior. We had decided to do this performance on a whim; invitations were extended by word of mouth through the corridors of Wayne County High School. Before we knew it, the choir had grown to nearly forty people and was loaded with talent: singers, keyboardists, organists, drummers, dancers, you name it! I had been entrusted with the assignment to direct the choir. My job consisted of teaching parts, perfecting arrangements, and giving direction during the performance. I loved my role! But me as the lead singer? Uh-uh. No way.

"What are y'all talking about?" I said. "I can't lead this song. I'll *direct* it, but we'll have to find someone else to lead!"

The last time I had performed in front of a crowd had been in grade school when I sang Whitney Houston's "Greatest Love of All" at my cousin's kindergarten graduation. In my opinion, that was a "kiddie" performance I had buried deep in the sea of the forgotten. I was completely perplexed as to why the group members were asking me to sing lead, but they remained persistent. I eventually agreed. Somebody needed to step up and do it.

The church sanctuary was packed with around two hundred people. Our concerts had become a big deal in our community. These encounters provided an outlet for worship and entertainment on nights that normally would have been spent watching reruns on TV or talking on the phone to pass the time. There wasn't much else to do! There were so many students in our choir, and often their entire families came out to enjoy the concert and support them.

The song I was being pressured to lead was "Now Behold the Lamb," written by Kirk Franklin and originally led by Tamela Mann. The mere fact that this was a Tamela Mann song was an intimidating thought. Her voice is packed with power, authority, and precision. Our group sang a lot of songs written by Kirk Franklin; I'd venture to say we sang his whole collection, top to bottom!

I stood in front of our choir and the congregation as the music began to play, closed my eyes, and belted out, "Now behold the Lamb, the precious Lamb of God."[1]

With my eyes tightly shut, I lifted my voice. It felt as natural as breathing. I always knew I could sing, but I didn't believe that it was my calling. Failing in front of others was a big fear for me. But I simply let go of that apprehension and sang the song, even in the face of fear. It didn't feel like a performance; it felt like purpose!

I'd never dreamed of being the one in the spotlight. I had been extremely comfortable with my background roles. But this moment revealed both to me and those in the room that there was more in me I needed to discover!

When I opened my eyes at the end of the song, I saw a room overwhelmed by God's presence. People were bowing. Hands were lifted. Faces were full of tears. I looked over at my parents, locking eyes. I believe we all knew this would be the beginning of a journey destined by God.

But I felt confused. *What is happening here?*

I had been in many church services where the presence of God could be felt in a tangible way. I had sung in choirs my entire life. I had played the keyboard for many revivals and church gatherings. But this was different. This response didn't come from a crowd simply wowed by a good voice. This was more than that.

This was an anointing.

It felt like God had just opened a door and I walked right through it. I knew He was leading me to my purpose. I glanced over at my parents once again, and their expressions mirrored what I was feeling. *This is something special.*

This moment—this precious moment singing about the Lamb of God—was something we needed to stay in. We could not move from that moment. For a while after the song, people remained in worship.

I realized then that God had entrusted me with a special

gift, a gift that was greater than I could've imagined. Now I needed to take the gift and do His work with it.

I believe we all have gifts that are waiting to be unlocked with a simple yes. Sometimes the gift lies dormant until we awaken it. This can occur after a long season, but it can also come from a single experience. Our yes may come from a challenging moment or from one of insight where we suddenly have a glimpse of what really lies within us. Or maybe the yes is a reluctant acceptance of our gift because of the push of others; we need to pay more attention to the talents people see in us.

*　　*　　*

My childhood memories often come with a soundtrack. Songs were always being sung, whether it was by me or someone else in my family. Everybody on my mother's side loved to sing—my aunts, my cousins. On Christmas and other holidays when everybody gathered, we would all sing. We called ourselves the Jacksons of Georgia. So even though music was part of my life growing up, I was not the "chosen" singer in our family. If anybody would have been expected to have a musical career, it would have been Quita and Tesha, two of my cousins.

Quita and Tesha attended the same church that I did. Back then, it wasn't typical for churches to have multiple choirs, but our church had four: the senior choir, the adult choir, a teen choir, and a youth choir. Aunt Charlene, one of my mother's sisters, led all of them, so naturally it made sense that her daughters were musically gifted. My cousins had gorgeous voices then as well as now.

We loved to have church no matter where we were. At school, we gathered in the hall, singing church songs between classes:

I get joy when I think about what he's done for me.[2]

This is the day that the Lord has made;
we will rejoice and be glad in it.[3]

Living, He loved me; dying, He saved me;
Buried, He carried my sins far away.
Rising, He justified freely forever:
One day He's coming—oh, glorious day![4]

My aunt Linda was a history teacher whose classroom was located near where we'd gather in the hall. It never failed: She would hustle out into the hallway and disrupt our "church service" to scold us for being out of order. She would quote her translation of Ecclesiastes 3:1: "There is a time and a place for everything under the sun," she told us. "But this is *not* a church house—this is a schoolhouse!"

We would scurry out of the hallway with laughter and joy. We knew that she loved to hear us praising God, because it was what she and so many others had trained us to do. And our worship made an impact on the other students around us. We witnessed students being saved and converted because of our decision to be loud about our faith. We just couldn't help ourselves.

People knew I could sing. But here's a little-known fact that I'm sure you didn't know: I was a baller. That's right—I was the captain of our basketball team. Sports were a big deal in our family, and I loved being part of a team sport. I believe the lessons I learned from team sports play a vital role in my being the leader I am today.

Many of the girls on our basketball team were also a part of our community choir, so, of course, we had worship on the bus while riding to games. We all believe that Coach Daniels, who also grew up in our family church, secretly awaited our bus church services, even though she never showed it.

So, yes—a singer, a basketball player, and a pastor's kid. Being a PK meant that I did whatever my hands could find to do in ministry. I filled whatever need popped up: "Sure, I'll play the keyboard." "I'll teach Sunday school." "I'll clean the church." I would do anything.

But lead singing? It just wasn't a role I played until this one mind-blowing night. Everything changed after that evening when I sang "Now Behold the Lamb." There was a monumental shift. I started leading more and began to really cultivate my gift of singing.

*   *   *

Church has always been part of my life, and so has working hard. Before my father started his own congregation, we belonged to my mother's family church. For years, Daddy worked a career job at Rayonier paper mill in Jesup. It was only when I was in middle school that he left his job at the mill to go full-time in the ministry. My dad went through the ranks of church assignments, starting out as a brother and then becoming a deacon, a minister, an elder, the assistant pastor, and eventually the pastor and bishop. He was serious about God's church: very committed, always forging forward, always being an example to me, my brother, and so many others.

Dad was born in Screven, Georgia, a small town about fifteen minutes outside of Jesup. Once reaching middle school age, all the kids who lived in Screven were bused over to Jesup for school. That's where he met my mother, Bertha Lockley, when she was thirteen years old. Soon after, the two started dating, and they remained together for thirty-eight years of marriage.

My father spent many long days at the church, but one of his creative outlets was building. He was a carpenter, just like Jesus! He loved to work on projects, and many of them he engineered himself. It was nothing for us to come home and see new additions to the house that Dad had just built. "I'm going to turn the garage into a sunroom," he told us one afternoon before starting to work on it. That's exactly what he did: He renovated our garage and made it into a beautiful sunroom for our family to enjoy, and then he built an additional garage onto our house. Even when he wasn't working at church, he was constantly working on something. That hard-work ethic was something I grew up watching and later found myself practicing, which I believe helped me cultivate my gifts.

Many people have shared that when they hear me sing, they feel they are experiencing a mixture of preaching and singing. I agree. After ministering at Lakewood Church in Houston, Texas, Pastor Joel Osteen rushed onto the stage, grabbed my hand, and stated, "It's like you're singing and prophesying all at the same time."

Led by the Spirit and after realizing the gifts God had given me, my dad tried even harder to foster the communicator in me. So instead of focusing on having me sing, he would put me up to preach. "I want you to teach this class," he would say. He saw that I had the gift of singing, but his actions revealed that he knew there was something more important, more foundational to cultivate. I can imagine what was going through his mind at the time: *I need you to have a foundation assured, Tasha. I need you to know the Word of God. I need you to know how to articulate and communicate it well so that when these doors open, you're not just singing songs but you have a revelation about what you're singing.* He knew that doors were going to swing open one day, so he pushed my character and my relationship with Christ.

"Baby, you really have to stay at the feet of Jesus now," Daddy told me. "God is up to something special."

Of course, I didn't realize all that at the time. I didn't understand what he was doing and why he was pushing me into leadership in the church. But he was showing me the things that I walk out now in my life. Even after I found success in the music industry and signed to a label and was winning awards, he always had the same message.

I would call him and say, "Hey, Daddy, there are going to be thousands at the concert tonight."

"Do good, baby," he'd reply. "Talk to you later. Stay at the feet of Jesus."

In the same breath, I could tell him I was preaching at a small church up the street and that would excite him even more than my singing at the White House. He realized that knowing God's Word would keep me grounded.

*   *   *

My dad wasn't the only person who knew those doors would one day open for me. Perhaps even more than him, it was my mom who believed in the anointing God had put on my life.

Because she grew up attending a Pentecostal church, where oftentimes there was lots of celebration and dancing, my mother would always be the one in tears. She was an intense worshipper. During the praise moments, she would be crying with her hands lifted to the heavens. Even though doing so wasn't very popular in the church that I grew up in, she was passionate in her worship. She had a job for thirty-eight years working at Fort Stewart, a military base in Hinesville, Georgia. Sometimes once she got home, my mother would just sit in her car in the garage and weep while singing and listening to worship songs.

After my experience of singing in front of the choir, Mom came in one day and revealed what she had just seen from God. "Tasha, the Lord just showed me your name in lights," she said with eyes full of emotion and tears streaking down her face. "He told me that people will know your name before they know your face."

I wasn't sure how to respond. My mind said, *Okay, that's crazy,* while my heart said that I believed her. Mom was the one who decided to act on my talents.

That moment when I received my first Grammy, people knew my name and knew the song, but for many, that was their first time seeing my face. It wasn't until I mounted the stage, adorned in an electric-blue ensemble that demanded attention, that people realized, *Oh, she's the one who sings*

"Break Every Chain." Mama knew doors would open, so she acted on that revelation and began to prepare me, as well. My mother believed in my eighteen-year-old self so much that she became my "momager" and began to drive me up and down the coast to sing at churches and events.

Back then, she had a white Toyota Sequoia, one of those oversized SUVs that could fit eight or nine passengers. (I believe sometimes we would squeeze in about ten.) Mama would drive me and some of the same teens from Sounds of Harmony choir to churches that invited me to come. Bubba, Ramon, Paul, and Shamar became my personal musicians. My cousins Tesha, Shania, and Asha would sing background as we performed at churches on the East Coast, going between Jacksonville and Orlando in Florida, and from Savannah to the Carolinas. My mom would pack little snacks and sandwiches and drinks in the Sequoia, and then off we would go.

My parents believed in me so much that they spent their money helping me make demos. I created a demo of the CeCe Winans song "Alabaster Box," and we sold it everywhere we went. People were buying it. It was a big deal on the East Coast!

*   *   *

If you can't tell by now, my parents were gung ho about their kids. They were going to do everything in their power to make things happen for us. They had seen God's hand on my life and wanted to prepare a way for my future in bringing our worship to many others. But they also wanted to teach me some valuable lessons that would train me for the rest of my life.

When I think back to my mom driving eight and nine hours in a car with all of us aggravating kids, it's obvious that she believed in us. She showed me the value of hard work, which is one of those foundational principles my parents laid down for me that I live by still today. It feels so old-school: riding in a car from venue to venue, performing songs, and gaining fans one at a time. The rise of social media and overnight pop sensations has changed the musical scene. But what I saw was that hard work and long hours and persistence pay off.

The other foundation—the most important one—was the foundation of family, the value of home. Yes, ministering God's Word and seeing lives changed is an amazing thing, but when it's all said and done, family has to come first. And if I can't minister to my family, I can't minister to anybody. That's what Mama and Daddy were teaching me as they poured into my life. It starts at home with your family. It starts with knowing what your faith means to you. And then you walk it out through hard work, prayer, and commitment.

Just recently, I was asked what advice I would give to an up-and-coming talent. That type of inquiry is always challenging for me because people truly want a cookie-cutter answer. The truth is, there is no magical formula. My response was, first, change your desire. Don't desire to be a rising star; desire to be the best you are called to be today! If that's singing in the community choir, do it with heart and passion. If that's teaching a Vacation Bible School class, make it so your students never want to leave. If that's ferrying your kids to and from activities, find a way to influence them in a positive way. If that's coaching a loud and wonderful basketball team, lead the players with energy and excitement. Each step on the journey of life is an important one.

There are no wasted steps. Overcoming my fear of having to lead a song in my teen choir was possibly one of the most vital steps toward my Grammy win. But even more important than that, it propelled me in finding God's purpose for my life. After we uncover those gifts that God has placed inside us, we need to unveil them to the rest of the world!

DO IT ANYWAY

Ask yourself if there is something you've been wanting to try but have held yourself back from based on a preconceived idea of your limitations. Sometimes you will never learn what you are capable of until you allow yourself space and grace to test your skills. Our greatest gifts and talents are realized just beyond our comfort zones. Pray and invite God to help you dream and envision what your future may be like if you overcame this limiting fear.

Don't let your comfort zone and preconceived limitations stop you from finding your God-given potential; do it anyway.

2

IN PREPARATION

The light rain felt refreshing as I locked the front doors of the store, knowing I would be back to work tomorrow at noon. The neon sign for Video Warehouse glowed above me. My evening shift had been busier than usual; it was a good night to stay indoors and enjoy a good movie.

I climbed into my car and exhaled. It felt good to finally be off my feet. Echoes of the question I had heard all day rang in my head: "Do you have any returns of *The Incredibles?*" The hit movie of 2004 had recently been released, and it was too popular to stay on the shelves. As the store manager for Video Warehouse, I was responsible for monitoring the fast-moving rentals.

It was 2005, and I was living in Jesup. My college days were over (at least for the moment). After high school graduation, I had gone to Clark Atlanta University for a year, then had transferred to Albany State for another year until eventually coming back home. Because I had worked at another video store called Movie Gallery during my senior year, finding a job at Video Warehouse had been easy. (In our smaller town, the store was the equivalent of a Blockbuster.) I enjoyed working there, especially since I got to see family and friends of the city pop in and out of the store. But liking my job didn't mean I felt fulfilled.

I knew there was a greater calling. There was a much deeper desire.

In the quiet of my parked car, the drizzles of rain tapping on the windshield, I turned on my car stereo and began playing the compact disc that had been played daily through my car speakers for months. I had the same song on repeat, speaking these words over my life: "I was created just to give you all the glory. I was created just to worship and adore thee."[1] The song "Created to Worship" was off the album *All Day* by William Murphy. I felt that this song was written for me and about my life and calling. I listened to it every day as a reminder that my current situation wasn't my final destination.

The song kept me grounded and focused. I would encourage myself daily: *Tasha, you may be working at Video Warehouse right now, but that's not all God has in store for you. You were created to worship. You were created for so much more.*

As I lifted up my voice alongside Bishop Murphy's, tears streamed down my cheeks. I gently wiped them away with a renewed hope in God's promises over my life. I knew who I was and why I had been created, and for the moment, that was enough.

At the time, I was still traveling up and down the coast on weekends when invited to sing at church anniversaries, youth services, conferences, and concerts. I hadn't forgotten the word my mom gave me about how she had seen my name in lights. She'd said, "People will know your name before they know your face." I wasn't sure how God was going to do all the things He had promised me over the years, but I believed He would. Ultimately, I loved to worship and I loved to lead other people into worship experiences.

After moving back home from college, I worked at Video Warehouse, performed on the weekends, and also began helping my father in ministry at my home church. My first initiative was to launch the worship team. Keeping in mind that our church was accustomed to a more traditional devotion experience, I was very gentle in my approach to this drastic change. The devotional worship experience was normally led by a deacon who would stand before the congregation and outline a hymn. After singing the hymn, he would open the floor for anyone in the congregation to share a song or testimony that was on their heart. These devotion experiences had been super effective and were part of the foundation of the traditional Pentecostal Holiness Church, but I really felt strongly that the structure and intentionality of a new worship experience would help lead our church into a deeper encounter with God. Daddy was a tad reluctant when I introduced the concept to him, but because he trusted my heart and my anointing, he released me to launch the worship ministry and build the worship team.

Building the team required lots of time, patience, study, and prayer. Back then, I had no clue what worship leading would look like for me, so walking it out daily was a new, refreshing experience. I loved it. (I still do!)

God had a plan for me. Those few years I was back in

Jesup, He was preparing me for something bigger, something better. I longed to see where He would take me, but I trusted in His process. I believe that the seasons leading up to the promise are just as important as—if not more important than—the promise!

*　　*　　*

That year, my father felt that we should attend a leadership conference being held at New Birth Missionary Baptist Church in Atlanta. This leadership conference would become a kairos moment, a time when God's purpose would be revealed to me. It was at this conference where God would give me clear instructions about my next move.

You have four months to move to Atlanta.

This made no sense. Internally, I was kicking and screaming! *Why Atlanta? Why now? This can't be happening, Lord. I'm comfortable in Jesup. I love my church. Dad and I are working great together in ministry.*

Isn't this just like us? We cry and pray to God for more. We ask Him to trust us with greater. Then when He opens the door and gives the instruction, suddenly we are paralyzed by fear and doubt.

We see this often in Scripture, but one character who stands out the most is Moses. Moses was called and anointed to lead God's people to the promised land, but even after receiving reassurance from God, he feared that his speech impediment would hinder his effectiveness. Moses was worried about his physical flaw, but it was his unbridled emotional flaw of anger that caused him to forfeit his access into the promised land. Just like Moses, we often focus on the external thorn, when the real issue is much deeper and could possibly be more detrimental to our success.

Along with leading praise and worship, I was also the youth pastor at the church. Our youth ministry had been growing by leaps and bounds, so why would God want me to go to Atlanta now? What possibly awaited me in that big city?

If there's one thing I know now, it's that we have to trust God in the fog. And life gets foggy a lot. There are times when God wants us to act on faith—to hear from Him and just go. So that's what I did. Four months to the day that I heard God tell me to move, I drove four hours to Atlanta with luggage in my car even though I didn't have a place to live or a job. I was moving from a town where I knew almost everybody to a major metropolitan city with around five hundred thousand residents. My cousin Quita lived there and was gracious enough to allow me to live with her for a while. That Sunday, September 17, 2006, I attended the inaugural service for a new church. The dReam Center Church of Atlanta had been started by none other than Bishop William H. Murphy III, the same person who, for an entire year, had been leading me and reminding me of my purpose.

As I walked into the packed service, the worship ministry team began singing a song that would later become my life's prayer. I later recorded this song—"For Your Glory"—on my *Grace* album, released in 2013. That song topped the charts, becoming a *Billboard* number one song that still blesses countless people to this day.

The team sang, "I wanna be where You are, gotta be where You are."[2] As those words rang out all over the congregation, I could hear God ask me a simple question: *Even if it makes you uncomfortable, do you still want to be where I am?*

I lifted up my hands and answered, "I wanna be where You are."

That Sunday, I was the one and only person to join the dReam Center Church of Atlanta.

I love how Bishop Murphy tells this story. He was Pastor Murphy then, and that Sunday, after holding his first service, he had gone home feeling confused and disillusioned: *God, why would You have me launch this church only for one person to join?* And he always ends the story by saying that you never could have told him that the one person who joined would be Tasha Cobbs! But here's the part that always gives me chills. At the same leadership conference where God told me to move to Atlanta, Bishop Murphy had been on the platform at that conference leading worship. That very night, God told him to start the dReam Center Church.

God spoke to both of us at the same time in the same room. We serve an intentional God!

When I arrived at the dReam Center that Sunday and heard "For Your Glory," I knew it was one of those moments when you just have to trust God's voice. I still couldn't see what was happening and why I was meant to be there, but I knew I had heard from God. A few days after joining the church, I got a call from Pastor Murphy.

"Okay, so you're the only person who joined this week," he said with a chuckle. "I need you to tell me your story, 'cause you've *got* to be somebody."

So I shared my story, which, at the time, felt more like a short story instead of a novel. It was a story that was still being written. A tale with no definite conclusion as of yet. A journey still very much in motion. I explained the moment in church when I sang "Now Behold the Lamb" and how I had been visiting churches up and down the coast. I shared how I would listen to his songs whenever I left my shift at Video Warehouse and how much they ministered to me.

"There is a grace on my life for worship," I explained.

* * *

God is about to do it. You know what it is. You just have to keep trusting and believing Him. God has a purpose for the season you're in right now. We have to trust His plan. Don't give up in the middle!

After joining the dReam Center Church, I realized it was important for me to immediately connect with the worship ministry. Though I knew I had a calling to help build and cultivate the team, it was key that I waited on God's timing and His divine setup. There were other leaders in place whom I was honored to serve during that season. One Sunday, after I had been there for about six months and served in the background in whatever capacity I could with worship, Bishop Murphy called on me.

"It's time," he said before the Sunday morning service.

I stood before the congregation with my eyes closed, just as I had done leading our community choir, completely focused on God and God alone. I prayed, *Lord, if I find favor in Your sight, Lord, please hear my heart's cry.*

That's right—I sang "For Your Glory."

Little did I know that I was singing a song that one day I would have an opportunity to introduce to the world, and it all started in front of a small church family of worshippers who simply longed for the presence of God.

> *For Your glory, I will do anything. Just to see You, to behold You as my King.*[3]

When I finally opened my eyes, I saw Pastor Murphy at the altar, weeping and bowing in a posture of worship. The rest of the church had similar postures. There it was again: The scene mimicked the experience at Bennett Union in my hometown the night I led "Now Behold the Lamb."

That moment, leading "For Your Glory," will forever be an unforgettable one for me. It was when I put my complete trust in God's plans. He had been too faithful, too consistent, too real for me to ever doubt His hand on my life again.

Soon after this, transitions were being made in leadership positions at the church. Pastor Murphy decided to assign me the position of worship leader. I had the sound for our church, but more important, I had a heart for the vision of the ministry. The timing was right. Pastor Murphy knew it. I knew it. Soon he shared with me what God had revealed to him concerning me.

"God told me to take you on the road with me and teach you everything He has shown me," he said. "I'm going to show you everything. Take the meat. Spit out the bones."

After I had been in Atlanta for six months, my father went there to give Bishop Murphy his blessing. "This is my daughter, and I trust you with her," Dad told Bishop Murphy. "I believe I've taken her gifts as far as I can take them, and now I'm passing you the torch."

This is why I refer to Bishop Murphy as my spiritual father. He was traveling around the world, so he explained that God wanted him to take me on the road with him.

Bishop Murphy had a vision for our church like I'd never seen up to that point, especially in a predominantly black church. Bishop Murphy saw a worship team as a choir of worshippers. He saw worshippers spread out all over the stage. This concept is common now, but it was very foreign then. I'd venture to say that Bishop Murphy is one of the founding fathers of the worship movement in the predominantly black church. He was bringing about the movement when it wasn't popular. His heart has always been for our community to experience a deeper encounter in the presence of God. He has always pushed us beyond emotion into a spiritual encounter. He trained me to dig deeper and expect more.

"I hear a sound that is all things to all people." When Bishop Murphy said this, he meant that we were going to create something that was relevant to everybody.

"When people walk into this church, regardless of where they come from, I want them to leave having experienced something that feels like them," he told me.

He wanted everybody to feel as though something about this service made them comfortable. And I took those lessons and put them into my songs. I wanted everybody—no matter where they came from and what kind of life they've had—to be able to relate to my music. That was my heart behind those first songs, and it just worked. It wasn't conjured up and it wasn't some well-thought-out scheme; it was really me saying, *This is who I am. This is how I sing these songs in my house.* I could take the most popular worship song and put a little gospel in it. That's how I presented it to the world. Little did I know that that's what people were waiting for. That was such a blessing, and it's *still* such a blessing!

At the time, this idea was mind-blowing to me. Nowadays, we see many examples of this way of worshipping, but back then, especially in the black community, it was not the format or the formula for services. It was the beginning of a shift in the black community with the sound of worship.

For me, it felt like a tsunami of creative ideas and passion suddenly got unleashed. There were no set rules. There was no template. We would write songs in our rehearsals that we would sing the following Sunday. I didn't know anything about copyrighting songs. I just knew worship. And that is how everything began to explode! People would watch our services and begin singing our songs in their churches, all around the globe. This was way before the pandemic and people attending online church. People would go home and watch our services and start to mimic that style of worship in their churches. We saw it all over the world as we traveled. Pastors shared that they had been watching our church and that they would have their worship ministries studying our methods.

"We just shared this song with our church," they told us. "Where did it come from?"

"We just wrote it on Friday," I explained.

We knew God was blessing what we were doing. Bishop Murphy gave me the grace to grow. He loved to introduce me as his daughter Tasha Cobbs, "a worship bridge to the nations." He was very transparent with mentoring me. So much of who I am is connected to who he is.

No one could've ever told me that all this—singing worship songs on a rainy night while driving home from Video Warehouse—was preparing me for something much greater than I could've ever imagined. I was focused on perfecting my assignment and responsibilities, but God was preparing me for greater!

DO IT ANYWAY

Do you feel stuck in your life and not sure where you're going? Amid the busyness of life, can you hear God talking to you? You have to remember to trust Him in the fog and act on faith when He wants you to get up and *go*! You need to go before Christ and pray, *I wanna be where You are, gotta be where You are.* Surrendering to God does not prevent you from moving forward; it prepares you to be ready to move whenever God calls on you. Even if the direction you're headed seems crazy, do it anyway!

3

IN THE HEAT OF THE MOMENT

Give God a yes before you can think of a reason to say no. When I am faced with a task or an assignment that God gives me, that is the approach I try to take. Of course, I'm human. Sometimes I allow fear and doubt to speak too loudly, but most times, I'm postured to face God-given assignments with a yes first. In 2010, that was how my very first album came to be. Like so many things in my life, the idea seemed to come out of nowhere. But once I saw God's hand in it, I ran with it, knowing He was leading the way.

When Rachel James and Kim Sky asked me to have lunch with them one day, I thought they just wanted to have a girls' day out. But they had other plans! I quickly realized the meeting was a divine setup; Rachel and Kim were simply the mouthpieces God had chosen to use.

We had barely even sat down to order our meals before the girls launched their stealth attack.

"So, when are you going to do this album?"

The question came out of nowhere.

"What do you mean?" I asked.

They both looked at me with expressions that said, *You know what we're talking about.*

"Tasha, everybody is singing your songs," Kim said. "People are waiting on *you* to release these songs."

I knew people were singing my song "Smile" because Jonathan Nelson had recently recorded it, but that was the only one I could think of.

"What about 'Happy'? And 'Confidence'?" Rachel added. "You have a lot of songs!"

"More than enough for an album," Kim added.

I just sat there shaking my head. "I don't need any of that. Y'all know me—I just love to worship."

For the entire lunch, all they talked about was this nonexistent album. I laughed at the idea and told them they were crazy, but deep down I couldn't shake the seeds they had planted. These were trusted voices in my life, and there was no reason for them to try to convince me to do something crazy. This notion from Kim and Rachel of an album was so heartfelt and real.

It is key to have people in your life who can be trusted to push you into purpose without them having a personal agenda. People who support your success when there's no benefit in it for them.

Was I avoiding the very idea of making an album and building something out of these songs? Maybe. I've learned that any time I run away from something in my life, it comes from a sense of fear: mainly the fear of failure. And it goes back to the never-ending battle inside us between fear and faith. While I'm usually able to take these thoughts captive, at the time, I was struggling. My friends must've been think-ing, *We have to say this to Tasha, and we have to say it now! People are singing her songs around the world, and she's missing her opportunity.* Looking back, I think I *was* missing it!

Here's something I deeply believe: It's so key to have the right people in our lives at the right time.

Something sparked inside me. For the rest of the day, I thought about that lunch date. I replayed it in my head, and I remembered the encouragement from Kim and Rachel. Their enthusiasm and firm belief that those songs *needed* to find a home on an album spoke to my soul. I tried to avoid thinking about it too much. It was too big of an idea, too daunting. I didn't know the first thing about recording an album. I just needed to go to sleep and forget the conversa-tion ever happened.

My spirit, however, would not let it go. The idea tortured me all night, keeping me awake, igniting a new passion. Soon I sprang out of my bed and went to find my laptop. I needed to document my thoughts. There was no point of reference for how I would realize the ideas that swarmed inside me. Yet as I began to write, a project began to take shape.

Maybe Rachel and Kim are onto something. Maybe this is my next step toward purpose.

* * *

Here's the amazing thing: The songs were already written. By 2010, they were alive and being sung and shared by so many people. But sometimes in life, we need others to help us see the gifts that are right in front of us—the gifts we have inside us and the gifts we are meant to share with others.

The dReam Center Church was part of the Full Gospel Baptist Church Fellowship. Our reformation of churches would gather yearly for the international conference, and thousands of people gathered from around the world for this five-day conference. At some point, I grew confident enough to share the songs that had been written during our rehearsals and worship experiences at the dReam Center. The worship team learned the songs and sang them at the conference; then attendees would go back and sing them at their local churches. That was how people began to know the songs and how they began to filter throughout the country and even the world.

The first inkling I had of this came when Jonathan Nelson, a well-known gospel artist and 2006 Stellar winner for Song of the Year, reached out to me one day. I was shocked hearing his voice on the other end telling me he had heard my song "Smile" and wanted to record it. My jaw dropped. We had only sung it at our church and the conference, so I was honored that he would ask. Of course I agreed to have him record it. The song would be landing on his *Better Days* album (which released in 2010) and recorded in front of a live audience. There was no way I was going to miss this monumental moment, so I gathered up enough money to secure a flight and hotel to Fort Lauderdale, Florida. It was surreal standing there in a theater hearing thousands of people sing a melody and lyrics that had been birthed from my heart.

More and more people were coming to know and love these songs written during my personal worship encounters and our rehearsals. My heart was grateful; that was why the songs had been created. I had no grand plan for them other than for people to be blessed by them. My dearest ministry passion is for the local church. I love to see God's people grow, develop, and walk out purpose. I love the community and the family environment of the local church. These songs were manifestations of that love and community. I never expected anything grandiose to be done with them; they were tools for our local encounters.

That's the beautiful thing about a community: Sometimes it takes others to help us see the clear truth that everyone else sees in us.

*   *   *

I was already writing songs and creating arrangements, so making an album was just a matter of documenting it all—putting it on wax, as they used to say. No big deal, right? I just needed a plan.

Remember, I didn't know the first thing about creating an album. Google would probably know, though. I went to my computer and began to search online: "How to produce an album." "Easy steps to recording." "How much does it cost to create an album?" "How to upload music to iTunes." "Live recordings for dummies."

I was surprised by how quickly and easily I listed and organized my ideas. It was as if I had been carrying these blueprints with me for years. As midnight came and went, I continued detailing a plan: the playlist of songs on the album and the order they should be in, the choir that would accompany me and who would sing background vocals, the musicians who would make up the band, and who would produce the project.

Did it matter that I didn't know what I was doing? Not one bit.

Did I want to sleep on these thoughts and revisit them in the morning? Of course!

Did I really want to do this? I wasn't sure!

The following day, I went to Bishop Murphy and showed him a fully developed strategy that I had typed out and printed overnight.

"What is this?" he asked, holding the document, which looked like a yearly report.

"I'm going to record an album," I said without a doubt in my mind.

He raised his eyebrows as he smiled. "Really?" Bishop Murphy knew me well enough to know that if I felt led to do something, I was going to do it. He encouraged me to follow my passion: "Oh yeah! Let's go for it!"

The crazy thing is that it really did happen overnight. Nobody had ever heard me talking about doing an album. Then I showed up with a multiple-page plan and the idea to make an album right away.

Vaughan Phoenix was the music director at our church. He and I had been writing and arranging songs together for years, so it only made sense to approach him about producing the album. He was skilled and creative. He understood my style of writing and the results I would be expecting. I couldn't help my excitement as I shared with him what I had in mind.

"So, we are going to do a *live* recording, and I need you to have it ready in two months," I said without a thought.

He laughed and shook his head. "You've lost your mind! That's not how this works."

Vaughan began to explain the process and how long things could take, but I wasn't really paying attention. The big kicker was that he was scheduled to be out of the country on the date I had designated for the recording. Fully committed to my plan, I told him he would have to figure out a way to record it virtually.

I am a person of my word. I had already told several people that the recording would be happening on a specific date, so I was determined to make it happen. I believe that our accountability to our word is the one thing that will get people to support, trust, and buy into our endeavors.

"This may not be how it usually works, but this is how it's going to work for me," I told him.

"No" has never been an option for me. I always figure out a way or make one. *This recording is going to happen!* I decided.

The greatest lesson my father could have taught me was to stay at Jesus's feet. It's not about being deep; it's about settling ourselves so we can hear instructions on how to move forward in life—because if we don't, we'll be all over the place trying to figure out how things can go wrong, how things can't work, what we can't do, and what we don't have the knowledge or education to do. When we submit all our flaws and our incapability at His feet, that's where we find strength. The power to move forward is in pausing before Jesus and allowing Him to encourage us. It's in hearing Him say, *I've given you what you need in order to do these things.*

There's a scripture that talks about God giving us the desires of our hearts. We often translate this scripture to mean that God will give us (physically in hand) what we desire. But maybe it should be translated to mean that the desires we have are placed in our hearts by God. So if He gave me this desire, I'm going to fulfill it with my best!

Of course, there was this little issue of how to pay for making the album. I certainly didn't have the funds. So, naturally, I went to the first person who came to mind.

*   *   *

"Daddy, trust me! This is gonna work!" When I first told my father that I wanted to record an album, he remained pensive as he listened to my ideas.

"I want you to be the executive producer," I told him.

His face lit up and he smiled. "Oh, I'd love that! Now, what does that mean?"

"Well, basically, how it works is that you pay for the album and then you eventually recoup your investment. And if it does really well, you'll be rewarded!"

In the end, my dad cleared out my parents' savings and funded my album. Just as they had always done for my brother and me, they gave all they had to support my dream. The truth was that my parents would have supported me no matter what; they were the type of parents who wanted the best for their children. But there was something else as well. I think they knew, just like I think Bishop Murphy knew. The same way my friends knew. Did *everybody* around me know that I needed to pursue this music thing, that putting out an album was a no-brainer? Maybe everybody just thought I was in denial. And I could have been.

Sometimes, choosing to avoid or deny a challenge can be a measure of fear of the unknown. Every day there is an internal battle between fear and faith going on inside us. I don't know if it was fear that had been holding me back; all I knew was that before Rachel and Kim invited me to lunch, I had never had the desire to record an album. And I *definitely* didn't want a record deal! That was my attitude at the time.

Then there's always the reality of seasons. Maybe the idea was never a thought because it wasn't the season for me yet. I believe we can sometimes grow so accustomed to and comfortable with where we are that we forfeit the blessings that come along with that new thing that may look scary and foggy.

Not only were the songs there, but so was something else.

I had my father's and mother's examples. Their work ethic, generosity, support, and surrendered willingness to follow God wherever He leads enabled me to move forward with plans for the album. I didn't know what I was doing, but I was surely going to figure it out!

Talent is one thing, but you have to match talent with tenacity.

Every artist must also be persistent in the pursuit of their craft.

Every gifted performer must also have perseverance to make it onto the stage.

Every skilled person needs a bit of resilience to steward their gift.

My first album was monumental, but it wasn't a miracle. It took a lot of hard work for it to see the light of day. I went after the task with everything I had, just like my parents always did.

My mom had always been gifted with administrative duties. She managed our pastoral-care team at church and was always organizing and giving structure. And although my father never started a business, the way he ran our church was similar to the way a business might be run: through administration, organization, and mentoring. Like my mom, my dad was an orderly person, so I had learned a lot simply by watching them in action. I never knew that trait was inside me until that night when I told myself, *I'm going to devise a plan.*

We captured the live recording at Higher Living Christian Church, in the outskirts of Atlanta. Vaughan was in Italy on a tour, so he Skyped with us at the church. This meant he produced the live recording from another country in another continent, something that is unheard of! Once the live recording was completed, it was time for the hard work. I never knew just how much effort was put into creating an album. Once he returned to the States, Vaughan immediately started the production process of the album. His job consisted of so many significant duties: scheduling and executing overdub sessions for the background vocalists and band, tuning and editing lead vocals, tuning and editing background vocals, tuning and editing instruments. Following that was the mixing process: merging all the recording elements together to create a beautifully balanced listening experience. While Vaughan was working around the clock to complete all his tasks, I was responsible for the marketing and album-release tasks. Again, I had never marketed an album. I had never uploaded anything to iTunes or streaming sites. Before my duties could be completed, I had to first teach myself how to do them. Hilarious now; scary then!

Research! Research! Research!

I researched how to put songs up on iTunes and CD Baby.

I discovered a site called TuneCore and learned how to up-load an album and schedule its release date. Via the social networking service Myspace, I found a graphic designer to create the branding for the album. I looked into companies that would package and print the album for distribution. Lastly, I needed a street team! I stand strongly on the belief that word of mouth is still the greatest marketing tool. I went online and searched for people who believed in me, people who would not only purchase the album but also encourage others to do the same. This was back in 2010. Facebook and Instagram were still new on the scene, and this was years before the invention of TikTok. With the help of Myspace, I created a grassroots campaign. To this day, I am amazed at the number of people who were willing to endorse that album with their support. I had thousands of flyers printed and shipped them to each street-team leader. I structured my campaign like a marketing ambush! All of us went to the parking lots of supermarkets, movie theaters, and malls to hand out flyers and spread the word about the album *Smile*.

Smile was an apt title for my first album. Joy and happiness flowed through these songs. The title invited people in. It provoked a desire and hunger for worship and personal time with God. During that period, I learned something about myself. I knew I was creative and had a heart for worship, but I learned how my creative abilities could be attached to not just my musical brain but also to the entrepreneur inside me. I discovered that I enjoyed the business side of things. I loved galvanizing the street team. Though the process was intimidating, I even loved learning the marketing side of it all. Off the bat, the album began to do well, especially considering that I was an independent artist and this was my debut.

Soon I began getting invites from everywhere, with churches from all over inviting me to come lead worship. It got so busy that I went to Bishop Murphy for wisdom on musical content for my performances. My album was out, but I still didn't have enough music to fill a complete set.

"I don't have a lot of songs. What am I supposed to do?"

"Mimic me until you find you."

So that's what I did. I would sing his songs just as if they were my own. The doors continued to open, so I just kept walking through them by faith, trusting God's plans.

*   *   *

Seems simple, right? I blinked and then birthed my first album. Of course, it wasn't so simple. It took many, many years before even the idea for an album came up. All those years of leading in my local churches and serving my pastors were seasons God was using to prepare me for something much greater.

My biggest blessing was something my dad instilled in me. It was the mindset that you don't fold at a task. You don't shy away and quit in the heat of the moment. You take it and you conquer it! And I think that's what I did. I saw God's plan and purpose, and then, before I could talk myself out of it, I went for it.

Sometimes in life, you can't trust what you see but you've got to know what you've heard. I knew at that lunch with my girlfriends that I had heard God telling me it was time for an album. But are we always ready to listen for His voice? He speaks in various ways. Sometimes His voice comes in the form of an unction—an undeniable urge to pursue or take action. Sometimes His voice comes in the form of a sign—something you might see that ignites a passion inside you to pursue a goal. Sometimes His voice is audible. Yes, God has a voice. The Bible refers to it as still and small. Most often, I've experienced His voice through others, maybe in the form of a sermon or message or through someone else's testimony. Or maybe through a loving confrontation like the one I experienced with Rachel and Kim.

No matter how He chooses to speak to you, make sure you're postured to receive what He's saying and take action.

DO IT ANYWAY

Pay attention to how God is leading you. What dream or divine invitation have you been suppressing because it feels too big or bold? You owe it to yourself to find out more about what it will take to make your dream happen. Look at the people in your circles and consider how God is encouraging you through their words. Begin asking for help in strategic ways; you might be surprised by where and how help arrives. Don't allow the feeling of inadequacy or a perceived lack of qualification cloud your vision. Do it anyway.

4

IN THE STORMS

There is power in the name of Jesus! You've heard me sing about it, haven't you? But it's the truth, and it never gets old to me. Cue the music:

*There is power in the name of Jesus
To break every chain.*[1]

I know this and proclaim this because for years I lived with chains weighing me down, invisible shackles that never made a sound. But those chains were broken. He broke every chain of rejection off me, and I know He can break the chains that bind you, too.

In 2010, after the release of my first album, I was busier than ever. Yet in the midst of ministering healing and freedom to everyone else, I found myself in the middle of a deep depression. I would get up before a crowd and inspire them with songs like "Happy" and "Smile," and people would leave having experienced freedom. I've witnessed God's power in ways unexplainable in moments of healing broken hearts through worship. God's presence would overwhelm us. Yet I would go back home and a darkness would greet me at my door and welcome me in. I found myself bound for days by despair. Very few people in my life knew about it.

My cousin Shanicka understood all too well what I was going through. We were roommates, so Nicka saw what things were like when I was home. For two or three days straight, I would stay inside our house with the curtains closed. I would be under the covers, plagued by a deep depression. At one point, things got so bad that Nicka packed her bags in exasperation.

"Tasha, I can't do this anymore," she told me.

My cousin was simply not equipped to deal with the heaviness that she felt in our home. She ended up spending a week with Pastor Murphy and his wife, Danielle, while I continued wading through the melancholy waters.

These sad feelings weren't something new; I had grown up carrying them inside. I always thought there was just something wrong with me. Even after I became the worship pastor at the church where I received so much love and acceptance from so many people, the feelings remained in me. I didn't understand what I was supposed to do about it. And in my isolation, the place the Enemy loves to corner us in, I would hear his lies spilling into my head: *Nobody really wants you. They only want you for your gifts and talents. If you were to die today, the world would find another Tasha. People would just move on.*

Logically, I knew none of this was true. I was surrounded by so many people who loved me for *me*. Yet this depression held me in solitary confinement. Not only did I hear these words, but I believed them. They made me lock my doors and suffer in silence. I didn't want anybody to see how much I was suffering.

But God saw me.

*　　*　　*

Sometimes in our sadness, God sends us a song.

After an event in Warner Robins, Georgia, I was driving our team back home. This wasn't unusual; everybody knows how much I love to drive. Since it was late at night, everybody was asleep while I was behind the wheel. I would often let my phone shuffle songs from different playlists on iTunes. That was one way I discovered new songs for the worship team. On this night, a new song began to play with simple piano chords before a woman started to sing in a plaintive voice.

"There is power in the name of Jesus."[2]

As soon as I heard these lyrics, I felt something break in my spirit. I immediately felt the tears welling up in my eyes. And despite what you've read so far in this book, I am *not* a crier. Crying is not something I do on a regular basis. But these weren't just tears for a song; they were the physical manifestations of the heaviness I had experienced for the past two years. While listening to those lyrics, I felt the heaviness being shattered. The sound began to break up the storm inside me. The sense of the world not wanting me or caring about me suddenly began to disappear. Pieces of the pain broke off of my life.

When I got home, I played "Break Every Chain" by Jesus Culture for several hours nonstop. And then for the next two weeks, it remained on repeat in my house while I was walking through this season. The song helped me experience deliverance and true healing.

One day, I knew a chain had broken when I heard God's voice: *Get up, Tasha. I want you to study the spirit of rejection. You've been calling this depression, but your depression is a branch off the root of rejection.*

So I began to study what this connection to rejection meant. At one point, I mentioned it to my therapist, and she confirmed it. "Yes, this is exactly what you're dealing with," she told me.

The more I studied and read about depression, the more I understood how it was attached to this theme of rejection in me. My issue was really one of self-rejection. It went back to my childhood, to growing up as a preacher's kid, to feeling as if people wanted and expected me to always be perfect. The PK. The do-it-all child. Little Miss Fix It!

I recalled the time when I was in elementary school and one of the deacons at our church came to me to ask if I could make sure his son did his homework and schoolwork. We were in the same grade! We were both children! With those weights of responsibility hanging over the head and heart of a ten-year-old, it was natural to feel the pressure of needing to be perfect. I didn't get to be flawed; I had to be perfect to carry all the gifts that I had and all the expectations others had of me.

As I entered adulthood, I carried those pressures and expectations with me. I was flawed and human and broken like everybody else, yet I was trying to live up to some unattainable goal of perfection. These feelings had been bottled up for years after my denying them, so much that I didn't know where to find the true Tasha in the midst of all the emotional debris. And I began to believe that the only thing people cared about was for me to get up and sing so they could be blessed.

All this was tied to that idea of perfection and the feeling of rejection. So one day, I woke up and made a promise to God that I was going to walk this thing out. I went to the mirror and stared at myself.

"I curse the spirit of rejection, and I receive the spirit of adoption," I told myself out loud. I repeated those words and made a vow to say them every day. Every single day. "I curse the spirit of rejection, and I receive the spirit of adoption."

As time went on, I felt myself coming more alive. I was growing stronger, emotionally and mentally. I was reciting the phrase to myself and declaring it over my life, and as I did, I felt God breaking those chains.

"I curse the spirit of rejection, and I receive the spirit of adoption."

The lies of the Enemy began to disappear the more I fed my spirit with the promises of God for my life. What I was exercising was a spiritual principle found in Proverbs 18:21:

> Death and life are in the power of the tongue,
> And those who love it and indulge it will eat its fruit
> and bear the consequences of their words. (AMP)

I have been *chosen*. God chose *me* as His daughter. Hand-picked.

*　　*　　*

I didn't know then the truth of what was happening. God had big plans to use me for His glory, but before I could move forward, I needed to deal with my demons of doubt. I knew what He was telling me, and it's what He's telling you, too:

> *You have to face this now, because if I allow you to walk through the doors that are coming without facing this stronghold, it is going to be one of the things that could cause major setbacks and disappointments in your life.*

If I didn't deal with my issues, they would absolutely show up again one day, possibly even more intensely. So as things began to get busier because of the *Smile* album, God allowed me to address my deep-rooted wounds, so much that I now feel comfortable sharing about it in public. What an honor it is to share the hope of Christ!

Now, it doesn't always feel good when you're walking out your testimony, but it's great to know that God can use it to help free other people. The healing didn't happen overnight, but every single day was a day closer to freedom. I would reclaim "Break Every Chain" and recite it to myself, declaring it over my life, time and time again.

When I first began going to therapy, I was wary of what it would involve. I had never gone and didn't know anybody who had—at least that's what I thought until I began to talk about it. At first I mentioned my therapy to only my family and friends. They were incredibly encouraging and supportive. They would constantly check in with me to see how it was going. They kept me safe but also made me accountable.

Some people—a lot of people—don't have that kind of support system, especially in our culture. Too many suffer in silence and isolation, and this is something we need to fix. Even though mental health is addressed on the news and media all the time, it's not talked about enough in our churches.

As I began to share my testimony, I realized that this isolation is something way more prevalent than we acknowledge. There are so many people, even those serving in leadership roles in the church, who are walking through this type of season, yet they're quiet about it. They feel as though nobody can relate to them, that nobody has ever been in this kind of season, that nobody understands these depths of darkness. For me, it went all the way back to the mask of perfection I felt I had to put on because I was a pastor's daughter. There was pressure to get the top grades and look the best. Then, down the road many years later, I looked back and half thought, half prayed, *My God, I don't even know myself! Who am I? I'm not just a singer, and I'm not just a preacher. There's more to me.*

We all have a fear of being vulnerable in front of others. That's why I've been willing and grateful to stand in front of people and share my own struggles and brokenness.

Every day, there is an unseen battle taking place, and it's over our minds. The Enemy tries to stop us from pursuing our purpose by attacking our minds and keeping us distracted. He wants us to focus on the darkness instead of fixing our eyes on Jesus. He wants to keep us from our destiny and from what God has called us to do. But we have to be intentional about looking to the hills, where our help comes from (see Psalm 121:1–2).

That's why every day, you have to take authority over your thoughts. That is what Scripture refers to as "the renewing of your mind" (Romans 12:2, AMP). I love the instructions given in Philippians 4:8, expressed so vividly:

> Summing it all up, friends, I'd say you'll do best by filling your minds and meditating on things true, noble, reputable, authentic, compelling, gracious—the best, not the worst; the beautiful, not the ugly; things to praise, not things to curse.

I soon got in the habit of filling my mind properly: *No. Not today! I'm not closing the blinds and hiding under the covers. I'm opening up the windows and letting the light in!*

We all have chains that bind us down in life. The only way to hear them fall is to allow God to break them.

*   *   *

While my healing from depression was beginning to take place, I woke up and saw my name blowing up on Twitter. Bishop T. D. Jakes had put out a message on social media saying that he was looking for the next voice in gospel music to perform at the Woman, Thou Art Loosed! conference: "You know who that person is? Tag me." My name began to be posted and shared, tweeted and retweeted, tagged and forwarded and used online in any other way it could be.

What is going on? I wondered when I saw the responses.

Suddenly here I was with all these pockets of supporters all around the world and a new album on the horizon. Thousands of people began to point to me. "It has to be @TashaCobbs," they all said in one way or another. They posted videos of me singing. I couldn't have imagined this type of response without seeing it with my own eyes. Eventually, someone from Woman, Thou Art Loosed! contacted me, asking for me to sing during the conference. After being asked, I knew what song I was meant to sing.

"Guys," I told my team, "we have to do 'Break Every Chain.'"

But the album wasn't finished. We were nowhere near completing postproduction for *Grace*. We still needed to go through the mixing-and-mastering process, something that usually takes about a month to complete. We had nothing produced to use as support—no stems, no tracks, nothing. And the upcoming conference in Atlanta was only two weeks away. I went to Vaughan and told him the situation.

"You gotta work a miracle here," I told him.

And that's exactly what he did. He went into the studio and created stems for "Break Every Chain." Meanwhile, the conference staff knew nothing about our urgent predicament. They didn't realize and probably never had a passing thought that I didn't have any music prepared yet. All they knew was that about 95 percent of the tweets Bishop Jakes had received were in favor of Tasha Cobbs and assumed I was ready to go. And by the time I arrived at the conference, I was exactly that: *ready.*

I was ready to walk into my next place of purpose.

The Sunday school lessons Bishop Jakes had started teaching at his church in West Virginia back in 1992 soon transformed to a life-changing women's conference that swept through the country. The first Woman, Thou Art Loosed! conference was held in 1996. When I went to the conference in 2012, held in Atlanta, thousands of women had gathered at the Philips Arena to celebrate God's promises and to fellowship with one another. After being introduced from the platform as the winner of the online contest for the search for the next big gospel music star, I climbed the steps to the platform and stepped into my favorite place: worship.

"Can you just lift your hands and release the name of Jesus?" I asked the women in the arena. "There's power in that name. Come on—there's power in that name. Don't stop saying it. Jesus. Jesus. We know where the power is."

I began to sing the song that had ministered to my soul so many times. I closed my eyes, just as I had done so many times before, and focused on God alone. This wasn't a moment about me; this was a moment to share a revelation I had personally experienced. So I led that beautiful congregation of women in this song of breakthrough. By the time I could get to "There's an army rising up," almost every single person in the room was on their feet, loudly declaring and shouting the words to the song.

The video on YouTube shows the power of this experience, but I don't want you to picture the young woman onstage with the soaring voice; I want you to see the girl lying in the dark with the covers over her head, warring with rejection. Once you can truly see her, then you can see the power of God working through her on the stage, leading others gracefully into the same healing: "I hear the chains falling!"

I could sing about those chains because I knew them all too well.

Thousands of women were going crazy, singing and crying. And even after I stopped singing, their praise continued. I couldn't help but laugh with joy. I loved it! Even when Bishop Jakes came out, the worship continued and the song kept going. I think back on that moment with gratitude that he had entrusted me with the platform God had trusted him with!

The next morning, Bishop Jakes's team reached out and asked me to come back to the conference to minister the same song. I was happy to go back and do it again. I had to travel that evening and couldn't sing at the conference that night, so someone else sang "Break Every Chain" in my absence. But I immediately flew back and sang for the rest of the conference. That day, people began to share videos of the performance, tagging me and talking about the song. Then I saw a moment that went viral: hundreds of women crowded at the Marta Station in Atlanta waiting to get on the train and singing "Break Every Chain." It was unbelievable!

Soon people started calling their radio stations and asking for the song: "Can you play 'Break Every Chain' by Tasha Cobbs?" I hear this is what every new artist *dreams* of! But here's the deal: I didn't have a single. We had nothing. We needed to get a single out *today* because all these women from around the world had left the conference on fire and were asking for this song.

The event was the beginning of a new season for me. The conference wasn't just a new chapter in my life; it was a complete life changer!

In 2022, I had the great opportunity to sing at the final Woman, Thou Art Loosed! conference. It was the thirtieth anniversary of the conference, and the ten-year anniversary of the moment I had been given to sing before thousands of women. I was asked to sing the final song on the final conference night. So before I ministered, I was able to take the opportunity to acknowledge Bishop Jakes for everything. "It's not very often that people would take a risk with their platform for something that's unknown. And I would be completely out of order if I didn't take this moment to say thank you."

More than a decade after singing "Break Every Chain" again at the Woman, Thou Art Loosed! conference, I am sometimes asked if I ever get tired of singing the song. Without question or hesitation, my answer is always a resounding no! I never get tired of watching people respond to this song. To the power of God. I never get tired of witnessing chains being broken off people's lives, because I know how it feels! I believe I can minister it the way that I do because I experienced it first. I felt the weight of those chains before singing about them. And I will always remember the freedom that washed over me as our team and I drove back home that night in Georgia. The handcuffs on my heart were unlocked, and the shackles on my soul were lifted. I felt I could breathe again, that I could see a glimpse of God's light in the darkness. And that is what happens to others as well: Pieces of their pain are torn off and put aside.

When we released "Break Every Chain" to the world, I had no idea what would happen next with the awards and the charts. I had no expectations of how it would affect the industry. I never expected any of that. I knew the song would touch people, but the full scope of that impact on the world and my life was just God's icing on this beautiful cake.

Will I ever get tired of singing "Break Every Chain"? Never. How can I when every single time I sing it, God's presence meets us in a new, unique, and exciting way? His change is freeing and refreshing.

That song is always a reminder that my chains are broken!

DO IT ANYWAY

Does the darkness sometimes seem too thick and overwhelming? Does despair follow you like a shadow? Never forget that you have been *chosen*. You have been handpicked by God. If you carry a heavy weight around with you, always remember that Jesus is there to break those chains. Do you believe in miracles? Trust that God will make a masterpiece out of your mess. Even when your faith seems so fragile, don't let the pain of right now force you to forfeit that miracle. Believe and do it anyway.

5

IN THE MIDST OF GRIEF

Grace is such a gift. When *grace* came to me as the name for my second album (my first with a label), I never imagined just how appropriate it would become for the season that followed.

The title and theme of the album was inspired after I heard a message on grace from Pastor Hart Ramsey in the summer of 2011. He had come to Atlanta one night, and in the middle of his message, he said something that really spoke to my heart: "I wish more songwriters would sing songs about how much God loves us. We're always talking about how much we love Him. Let's write songs about His grace."

I didn't hear another word in his sermon, because right away I took out my phone and began to pen lyrics to a song!

God loves me, adores me
Watches over me
You are for me[1]

That song became so real to me and became the anchor to the album. I felt convicted to put a spotlight on God's grace.

Even before we recorded *Grace*, I had already glimpsed the power of these songs. I knew they were life-changing and designed to bring people into worship. But I never imagined how God would use them. All the awards and accolades that came with *Grace* felt surreal, but I knew who the glory belonged to. This was all about His glory! I wanted to be intentional about releasing songs that directed all attention back to God. "Break Every Chain" is a perfect example. That song reminds us where our power comes from. It's in the name of Jesus! That's why I believe "Break Every Chain" became so infectious. When it first came out in 2013, people went bonkers whenever I began to sing it with the band and singers who traveled with me. The song was an anthem boasting about the power of God!

I had no idea that after such a mountaintop year, I would find myself unexpectedly thrust into such a dark, lonely valley.

*   *   *

"Tasha, your dad just had a heart attack. They want us to come home."

I stood in the living room of my two-bedroom apartment in Atlanta the evening after the Stellar Awards and stared at my cousin Shanicka in disbelief. At the time, she was working as my assistant, so everybody knew she was always with me.

Nothing could have prepared me for this news.

I sat on the couch in the living room, feeling very confused and challenged. *I just saw him. I literally just saw him a few hours ago.*

All they told my cousin was that my dad had a heart attack while driving and that the paramedics were working on him while he was still inside his vehicle. As Shanicka and I headed to the airport, I couldn't stop worrying and wondering what was happening with my father. It didn't take too long before my brother, Sharé, called me.

"Tot, he's gone."

We pulled over to the side of the road to process this awful news. The first words out of my mouth weren't laced with grief, however. They were words of praise and thanksgiving.

"Thank You, Lord. Thank You that You chose me to be parented and fathered by one of Your greatest gifts." The tears streamed down my face even as I prayed. "God, I thank You that for thirty-two years, I was given the opportunity to experience the love, the leading, and the teachings of such an amazing man."

Even now as I write these words and think about my father, the first thing I do before expressing any hurt or sadness is to say, "Thank You." Just like in those initial moments of knowing my dad had passed away, I reflect on the great man that he was. It's not just because he was my father. Fritz Cobbs exemplified, probably more than any other person I've seen, what it is to live like Christ. He lived out his faith in every way he could. It was awe-inspiring to see how he loved people beyond what they deserved.

When I eventually learned how Daddy had passed away, I was amazed at the way he protected my mother even in his dying. He had been behind the wheel of the car, and it would be expected that in the moment of his heart attack, the weight of gravity would've forced his foot to press down on the gas pedal, but instead he used his last bit of strength to lift his foot up off the gas so the car could coast into a ditch. No, not just coast—they floated into that ditch.

That's an example of the type of guy my father was. He would give his life to save his family, and he demonstrated that with his last breath. I can imagine him thinking, *It's not your time, so you're not going with me. I'm going to take my foot off the gas.*

After the car stopped, my mom ran across the street to a house to get help. My brother quickly arrived on the scene.

I wonder what my father saw in those last few moments of his life. I wonder what he felt. What were his thoughts? Our family talks about it often.

"He left me," Mom will say. In her mind, she believes he had an inclination that his time here on earth was coming to an end.

He loved God! He lived his life in a way that would bring God glory. I know it's a challenging thought, but the truth is that Daddy has received the ultimate reward. Because we're believers in Christ, heaven is our reward. We are living to live again. Sometimes I believe we adopt the customs of this world and forget that earthly things are not our reward. For years, anytime my father preached and talked about heaven, he would say, "If I ever get a glimpse, I'm not coming back."

When he said this, you just knew he meant it. It's a beautiful thing to want to be with Christ. That was my father's heart, and we knew it. Everybody knew it. Even now, some of the church members will say with a smile, "He always told us that if he ever got a glimpse, he'd go!"

Of course, we don't know for sure, but I believe that he

had a choice in the car that day and he chose Jesus! I think he got a tiny glimpse, and that was all he needed. He took his foot off the gas and guided the car to safety and then left us.

And I can just hear what he said: "I'll see y'all when you get here."

*   *   *

The following days after learning of my father's passing are still blurry to me. With everything that was happening in my life with "Break Every Chain" ringing out around the globe, people from everywhere began reaching out to me to offer their prayers and condolences. Everywhere I looked—I mean *everywhere*—there were blogs and magazine articles stating, "Tasha Cobbs's father passes." There were pastors and artists calling from all over the world. I literally don't know how so many people even got my phone number. I was grateful, yet at the same time, I was overwhelmed. I kept thinking, *Hey, I'm just Tasha from Jesup.* I couldn't believe how many people cared to reach out to me.

We wanted to try to keep the funeral service as intimate as we could, but that was kind of impossible. My mom didn't want it to be too long. I remember a weird moment from when our family was getting into the limo after the service. These women we had never seen walked up to the hearse and started taking pictures of us. We weren't on a runway; we were at a service to celebrate the life of my father. The people who were there to protect us made the photographers leave. All of us knew there was nothing glamorous about our family. We weren't celebrities. We just wanted a simple and private funeral.

I couldn't help thinking about the Grammy Awards coming up the following weekend. I had been looking forward to the event, and my father knew about my excitement. He had been continually encouraging me to attend.

"Daddy won't be with you in L.A., baby," he'd said to me several times. "But I want you to go. I want you to go anyway."

I would just laugh each time he'd say this because *nobody* expected him to fly across the country for any reason. We could barely get him to go across the street, much less to Los Angeles.

Days before the Grammys, my mom asked if I was still planning to attend them. "I think you should go," she said.

I still couldn't believe that Dad wasn't there to watch me, even if it was from the television in their living room. One of my biggest fans was no longer there to cheer me on in the background. He wasn't there to talk to on the phone, even if it was only for a brief pep talk. His smile wasn't around to give me the assurance I wanted and needed. But regardless of all that, I knew what he would have wanted.

"I'll go," I told my mom. "I know Dad wanted me to go."

By the time I arrived in Los Angeles, I felt smothered in grief. I could barely put two sentences together. I wanted to be with my family, to cry and grieve without strangers watching. I wanted to walk down my driveway, not a red carpet. I didn't want to answer questions from the media, nor did I want to put a smile on my face for the millions of people watching the show. But I remembered the words of my father: "Do it anyway."

So I did.

When the time came for one of the awards I was nominated for—Best Gospel/Contemporary Christian Music Performance—I sat there in the Staples Center, hearing them list off the other talented people in the category. When my name was called, I remained in shock for about twenty seconds.

There is no way this is happening. This is some kind of dream.

My astonishment lasted so long that it was getting close to the music starting to play. My cousin Shanicka, who was sitting beside me, gave me a sharp nudge.

"Tot, get up."

As I snapped out of it, bounced out of my seat, and walked across the stage, the moment still didn't feel real. I had never planned any of this. Recording albums and signing with a label and winning awards were not things I had grown up dreaming about. None of it was expected or imagined. But that's just like God. Ephesians 3:20–21 reminds us of it this way:

To Him who is able to do exceedingly abundantly above all that we ask or think, according to the power that works in us, to Him be glory in the church by Christ Jesus. (NKJV)

Being nominated for a Grammy was a lot to digest; winning one was inconceivable. I arrived thinking, *Let me go ahead and get this over with. I'm only here because Daddy wanted me to be.*

When I reached the microphone, I said the first thing that came to my mind. "This is solely dedicated to my father, who was one of the most amazing men to walk the face of this earth. Can you stand to your feet to celebrate my dad?"

The entire academy stood up and began to applaud him. What a remarkable moment in time to experience! Suddenly I no longer felt smothered by grief; instead, I felt embraced and comforted. Everything became real—even the fact that Tye Tribbett was the one who had presented me the Grammy. My father had a special connection with the legendary gospel artist at a leadership conference several weeks before the Grammys and came home talking about him nonstop, so much that I had texted Tye to ask what he'd done to my father. "My dad loves you!" I told him. So it was comforting for me to have Tye there onstage with me, understanding the gravity of this moment and knowing how my heart felt.

I couldn't help wondering if Daddy, up in heaven, knew this was all going to be happening. If somehow he helped set the whole thing up.

My father had left me with many lessons, and he was always a living example of forging forward despite the task ahead. In the midst of all my grief, I chose to get up and keep going. The standing celebration confirmed for me that God was still with me, that He still had a plan for me. A place had been prepared for me in the music industry.

Even though my greatest example of God's love was no longer with me, this love could be woven into the songs I shared with the world.

*   *   *

"Baby, stay at the feet of Jesus." That was another saying my dad loved to tell me anytime we spoke. Now that he was gone, those words especially resonated, transformed from a parental reminder to a lifeline.

Back home, after the bright lights and glamour of the Grammy Awards, I regrouped with my family and we began the process of healing. We have a very close family, and my father was the glue that held us together, so everybody was devastated. My mom, my brother, and I needed to figure out how we were going to move on from losing Dad.

My schedule at that point was crazy. I was always traveling, many times six days a week, touring and seeing the world. My father had been training Sharé as a pastor for the past year, but my brother and I had a conversation with Mom about the possibility of stepping away from ministry. I canceled a few upcoming performances and believed taking a break was the right thing to do.

I had kept one show at a church in California, fully accepting that I would soon not be performing anymore. There was an old song I felt moved to sing, a tune not even on my setlist: "Yes Lord, Yes," by Shirley Caesar. The words felt like familiar friends I was finally seeing again.

"I'll say, 'Yes, Lord, yes,'" I sang out. The verse is written, "With my whole heart, I'll agree,"[2] but I sang, "With my broken heart, I'll still agree."

In that moment, while I sang that song onstage, the Holy Spirit spoke to me clearly: *Running away from My presence is not the move to make, Tasha. This is the time when you run to the feet of Jesus, not run away.*

After the show, I hopped into the car to return to the hotel. I immediately called my mom and my brother. "We're doing this wrong," I told them. "We're doing this all wrong. We've got to get back to doing ministry. That's where our comfort is going to come from, and that's where our peace is going to come from."

I felt as though running away would have set us back in our grieving. I believe grief is purposed, but I also believe it's purposed for only a season. We walk our way out of that season of grief in different ways.

My mom and Sharé did what I asked. And my mother, after I told her my feelings, did something so very wise: She sent our entire family, including her sisters and my father's sisters and all my cousins, into therapy. Every week, we all got on a video call with a therapist. And this was before this method of communication was so commonplace in our post-pandemic world. No matter where I happened to be, I would get on Zoom or Skype with the rest of our family to do therapy together.

I truly believe God led my mother to set this up. Our therapist helped us compartmentalize our feelings and emotions so we could understand the different seasons of grief. I would encourage so many families to do this. I feel we lose our children in these dark places where they can't communicate how they feel and so they go off in an emotional spiral. Sometimes grief tears families apart; Mom saved many lives by having us go through therapy together. Her decision drew our family closer.

When we went back to the ministry, we were reminded of all the people my dad had influenced. Our family wasn't the only one that needed to heal after losing him. The church had lost their pastor. To most, my father was the only one they had ever known. He was a hands-on pastor, someone who called to check on them and attended their kids' basketball games and events. He was a father figure to many who didn't have fathers, so many of them needed help to grieve as well.

A year after my dad passed away, I was being interviewed and was asked about him. As we began to talk about my father, the interviewer made me see things in a different light.

"We are so proud of how your family exemplified how Christians are supposed to grieve," the interviewer told me.

I had never thought about that. We love to teach and preach that God is our peace, but it's very rare to have to live that peace out in front of the rest of the world. How are you going to act when you really feel the loss and the burden, when you are desperate for His peace?

Stay at the feet of Jesus.

We made that decision to run to His feet in front of the world. They were watching us, and I feel we represented Christ very well through this trying season.

Dad was watching us too. I know he was proud we kept forging ahead.

*   *   *

My dad's death hurt. There's no way to deny the pain I felt. Anyone who has ever lost a loved one can understand this. But there's an advantage we have as believers: the Holy Spirit! The Spirit is our comfort through every single one of life's situations. My heart hurt, but my spirit rejoiced that Daddy was face-to-face with Jesus. I was experiencing the peace that "passeth all understanding" (Philippians 4:7, KJV), the one that we had been preaching about all these years.

I had two choices: I could run away from Jesus and ministry, or I could run to Him. I chose to run to Him—to do as my father had always taught me to do and stay at the feet of Jesus. That is where I found the peace to cover me and keep me sane. That is how I still found an unspeakable joy in the midst of unimaginable tragedy.

Running to the feet of Jesus helped birth a greatness that God had entrusted in me. That greatness comes only from the Father. And know this: We all have greatness within us! When you're dealing with a tragedy, the pain goes beyond emotion; it's something that really pierces you to the core. I think in my grief, I found that my core was much stronger than I'd imagined. Not just my core, but my entire family's core. Mom never thought once that she would be able to live through all that, but now she calls it her 2.0.

When you have a tragedy that pierces you beyond what you can articulate, you find out how strong the Spirit is within you. Most people will say, "I didn't think I'd make it," but know there's something stronger in yourself!

When I look back on this season, I honestly don't remember much about it. It was a year full of victories in the midst of excruciating emotional pain; a year of "When I am weak, then I am strong" (2 Corinthians 12:10, NIV); a year of the peace that "surpasses all understanding" guarding my heart and mind (Philippians 4:7, ESV); a year of suffering with Christ and reigning with Christ (see 2 Timothy 2:12).

Every season, even the ones of victory, won't always feel good. But I lived to tell you today that God is working it for your good! I wish I could say that my dad's passing was the last time my heart broke because of loss, but you and I know that loss confronts us far more often than we want. From grieving a family member to grieving a part of our identity because of a major life change, the way to get through is still the same: Stay at the feet of Jesus.

For someone reading this, I know it feels like you're gonna die in the difficult season you're in, but I came through loss and grief to tell you that you won't. In my darkest season, God placed me on my greatest stage. How you handle this season, though it may be dark, ministers to someone who's watching. Be encouraged—it won't be this way always!

DO IT ANYWAY

What have you given up after tragedy has come into your life? Has the pain sidelined or stopped you from fulfilling the purpose God has for you? It's okay—sometimes even necessary—to pause good things to care for yourself and your loved ones during seasons of heartbreak. But today, spend time in prayer and worship and ask God if He is leading you to return to what you left behind. When those life-changing, hope-breaking moments happen and you find it hard to trust God and give Him the glory, do it anyway!

6

IN PURSUIT OF PASSION

Once I was able to break through my battle with depression, I found my purpose. It was more than merely singing and writing songs; it was also leading others to find their purpose. As "Break Every Chain" began to reach many parts of the world, there were social media messages and emails from all different cultures and nationalities reaching out to me. So many people were looking for guidance.

Purpose is a beautiful thing. I love to sing and I love music, but more than that, I love to see people flourish and find their God-given calling in life. Encouraging others to become greater at what they're called to do is one of my most important assignments from God, and it's one of my most precious gifts. I didn't know that when Bishop Murphy called me a "worship bridge to the nations," this is what he was referring to.

It wasn't until I witnessed the response to the release of "Break Every Chain" that I began to see that bridge for myself. It wasn't just a bridge between music genres but more so a bridge between cultures, nationalities, races, and all people groups. God began to give me a vision, but it at first seemed too big and too unlikely for my own eyes.

After the release of my first album in 2010, I continued to serve my church, and I started receiving emails, messages, and calls from worship leaders around the world asking the same question: "Can you mentor me?"

I couldn't imagine why they were wanting advice from me. I was still so young in my life and my career. What did I have to offer? I turned several of these requests down because I take mentorship seriously and knew that my schedule wouldn't permit me to spend the necessary time with them that I felt would be needed. In my mind, mentorship was tangible. Somebody needed to be present to touch you, to walk with you every day, to see you face-to-face. But the requests continued to come.

One day I came across 2 Timothy 2:15: "Study to shew thyself approved unto God, a workman that needeth not to be ashamed, rightly dividing the word of truth" (KJV). In essence, the verse was telling me that people could study me from wherever they were. I began to think of how I had studied under other people from afar, like the worship legend CeCe Winans. I was led to a great conviction: Who am I to deny people the ability to study my life's journey?

Unable to shake this vision, I decided to have a conference call where people could jump on and I could share my heart and experiences. Maybe people would call in, and maybe they wouldn't. But why not try something new? So in 2012, I had the first call, and 450 people phoned in! I couldn't believe it. In the back of my mind, I couldn't help thinking,

Are you kidding me? Why? What do y'all want to hear from me? I still felt like I was nobody special, but I had a special message to share with others. This was how the iLead Escape was created.

In the beginning, I invited different artists and pastors to call in and share their experiences—the good and the bad. The transparency during those calls was life-changing. People like Bishop William McDowell and Israel Houghton would phone in and mentor worship leaders from all around the world. It was truly priceless because it was free! Nowadays, people pay thousands of dollars for this kind of insight. You download an app and pay a monthly subscription for advice and wisdom from leaders. But our program didn't cost people a cent! People called in and received wisdom—not just worship leaders but everyone, from pastors to business leaders.

By 2014, we had grown to more than two thousand mentees around the world. The program grew so big in places like Africa and London that we had to have it twice in one day. People from around the globe would call in at three in the morning due to the time difference. Instead of inconveniencing them, we chose to add another session that would make it easier for leaders in their time zones. It would make for a long day for me and the instructors involved, but it was worth the work!

I still felt as though this mentoring program was an assignment that I could never walk out. Around this time, God gave me instructions to have our first in-person experience, the iLead Escape: Face to Face. Everyone would finally come together for an encounter in Orlando, Florida, where we could worship, receive impartation, and have fun and fellowship. More than six hundred worship leaders took the time to escape the challenges, complexities, and work of ministry to be refreshed in the presence of God and other leaders. It was fantastic!

Two years after our first conference, we had the second one in Birmingham, Alabama. This time we had more than twenty-five hundred register and show up! It was unbelievable to me how people continued to come. The night sessions were free, so we would have two to three thousand people in the room. We reimagined the typical panel and hosted what we called the "Tweet & Eat," where people would tweet in their questions for the panelists while eating their lunch.

There was one moment in particular that I will never forget. James Fortune, who's won multiple awards as a gospel artist, was hosting the panel. One of the leaders in the audience tweeted a question about mental health and suicidal thoughts. James politely asked if he could step out of his role as panel host so that he could speak to this question specifically. James was dealing with a very public divorce that most in the room were aware of. I'm sure there were those who had formulated their own opinions of the situation and possibly had turned a deaf ear to what he said. But there was something peculiar, something special, something anointed pouring from his heart that could be felt through his words. No matter how people felt about the vessel God was using, it was undeniable that James was being used by God.

Nothing could've prepared us for what God was about to do!

I felt that James had something to communicate and freed him to share as he felt led. James began to tell the room that he had left a bottle of Xanax on his nightstand at home and was planning to return home from the conference to commit suicide. His transparency as a minister and influencer not only broke the chains that were binding him but also motivated hundreds of others to experience breakthrough and healing. While sharing his testimony, James broke down. Standing close to him on the stage was his best friend and fellow gospel sensation Isaac Carree, who had no clue of James's suicidal thoughts. Isaac immediately rushed over to James and embraced him with the love of Christ.

I grabbed the microphone, feeling led by the Spirit. "If there are leaders in the room right now who are battling depression and suicidal thoughts, I want you to rush this altar," I boldly said.

As hundreds of leaders came to the stage, my heart broke. *God, what do You want us to do with this?* Here were leaders who had been suffering in silence. A deafening silence. This easily could have been James's or any of the participants' last time at the conference. But as those people ran to the altar, we ministered to them each individually.

From that moment forward, we have been intentional about ministering to the mental health of leaders who attend any iLead gathering. I vowed to God that I would not be silent about mental health, especially among leaders. So in 2018, when we hosted the iLead conference in Greensboro, North Carolina, I gathered a host of therapists to show up and offer their services free of charge. I announced that if someone felt they needed therapy sessions, they could schedule a time to sit down and meet a therapist at the conference. All they needed to do was text them and schedule it.

What had once been a phone call with fellow worship leaders in the country had now grown into a conference hosting thousands of pastors, leaders, and entrepreneurs. Along with the general worship sessions, we had classes for administrators and courses for those trying to get their business off the ground. Session topics included initiating self-care, managing burnout, and prioritizing a meaningful connection with God. In a time when pressures and expectations of leadership constantly derailed worship pastors and ministry-support teams around the world, the iLead Escape existed to equip leaders with the necessary tools to survive and thrive.

God never ceases to surprise us by doing amazing things with each conference! Even during the pandemic, when we had planned to have a conference in Greenville, South Carolina, we were able to offer instead the iLead Virtual Hang Out. More than seventeen thousand people registered and were able to watch Sarah Jakes Roberts, Kirk Franklin, Dharius Daniels, Priscilla Shirer, Brandon Lake, Brooke Ligertwood, and others. These leaders taught sessions and led worship virtually. For four hours, people watched online from their homes.

After the virtual conference, I thought surely it would be my last. I said, *Okay, God, we did it! Yay!* I envisioned that perhaps the next step would be much more advanced and personal, where we would have one-on-one or small-group experiences. But once again, the Lord told me to hold another conference. So in July, we hosted iLead 2023 near Atlanta. Every time we gathered, from the round-table discussions to the worship sessions, God did something so unique that we will never forget His grace! The encounters and experiences we had changed our lives forever. Praise God!

Is it scary to continue to pursue passion projects that you never sought to do in the first place? Absolutely! The iLead Escape is one of my babies that I'm super proud of, but it's always frightening going into another foggy assignment. If there's one thing I know about people, it's that they wait until the last minute to register. Sometimes we'll get close to the date and I'll think, *God, help us—nobody's coming!* Then the week before, a thousand registrants sign up.

You really have to take a leap of faith for the things in your life that matter the most, for the things that have the most influence on others. It's constantly a leap of faith with iLead, but people always show up. And I've had an opportunity to see its impact on people, with most of them growing tremendously as leaders. The program has transformed the lives of many aspiring musicians, entrepreneurs, and business leaders. I've had a chance to see some of the participants arrive seeming timid and shy and then emerge into leaders who now guide a congregation or team of people with boldness and clarity.

I've watched them grow because *I've* grown.

* * *

Mentoring is a way to help others as we work to better ourselves, share in our experiences, and pass on wisdom as we continue learning. Mentorship can establish the regular practice of looking back and seeing how far we've already come.

But here's some good news: You don't have to wait to become an expert to begin telling about what you're learning along the way. There is power in sharing your testimony with others and a sweet reward in knowing you have been part of someone else's journey toward their God-given dream. No lesson is too small. Every single thing you experience can turn into a lesson that's beneficial for the people you pour into. As a mentor, you can be pressured to focus on only the big moments and things in your life, but most lessons are learned in increments, in small experiences in life. Sometimes I look back and think of myself in ninth grade when my friends and I started a community choir. We asked around, and churches everywhere opened their doors and let us use their facilities to rehearse. That was the start of something special. That was the start of God showing me that there was so much more to my purpose. I was with a community—a community that kept growing. We worked together, grew together, and loved together.

I believe my father knew this about my singing. He understood that the singing was the *door* but not necessarily the house itself, and that's why he invested much more attention in my leadership skills. He knew there was more. He was thinking of what was to come. And that's what we need to always do as well. We have to stay grounded and watch how God will swing doors open in our lives.

My purpose is much more than just singing. Sometimes

it's about sitting in the background and experiencing the Spirit work through others.

With the iLead Escape, "Tasha the preacher" may preach at one of the sessions, but we have such an incredible variety of artists who come in and share worship through song that "Tasha the gospel singer" is never on the program with plans to sing. We have a talented worship team. And so many incredible speakers come to share their wisdom with everyone. My passion is sharing the tools I've used through the years to help me become greater at my craft—at being a worship pastor or a worship leader to different people.

Mentorship means so much to me. There are many stories in the Bible about mentorship, and I am fortunate to have mentors who help me navigate through life—people such as my dad and my mom and Bishop Murphy. It's been a blessing to see the development and growth of students like my goddaughter Breona Lawrence, whom I started mentoring when she was thirteen years old. When I saw that she had a great calling on her life, I took her under my wing. Now, more than a decade later, I can watch her lead worship and prayer in front of crowds of thousands. These things come full circle. There are a few leaders I've mentored over the years who are serving the Lord in amazing ways. I am proud of the part I had in helping them become what God called them to be.

There is something so spiritually fulfilling in watching someone be great at what God has called them to do. Every day is a chance to discover something new about ourselves or others. Learning is a lifelong process.

DO IT ANYWAY

Do you know your purpose? If you struggle to find it or feel as though you've drifted away from the passions you had years ago, ask yourself this: *What do I have to offer others?* Think about the conversations you've had with mentors—those people you respect and appreciate, especially because of the way they approach life. Think about those in your life who have meant something to you, who have motivated you. What have they helped you discover about yourself? When you find a passion that turns into a purpose, you find joy and direction in every possibility life brings. When you surrender that purpose over to God, even daunting or impossible projects become doable. Unshakable purpose propels you to unharness your fears and do it anyway.

7

IN BATTLING GIANTS

We all face giants in our lives—what seem like invincible enemies that show up every day to wage war against us. The battlefield is right in front of us. We can choose to step onto it and fight, or we can turn around and flee. Or maybe we can do the easiest thing and ignore the conflict altogether.

Let me encourage you—you are not alone. It doesn't matter who you are, what season of life you're in, or how big of a platform you might have. We *all* fight battles. We all face what Scripture calls a thorn in our flesh (see 2 Corinthians 12:7). It's a nagging reminder that, yes, we are human. For some of us, it might be a fight with our emotions or for our mental health. It might be an addiction or a relationship or a fear. And as much as we love miracles, everything won't have an instantaneous fix. Some things we have to walk out day by day by day by making better choices to overcome our battles.

One of *my* fights has been with my weight.

Around the time of the release of *Smile* in 2010, I had one of those wake-up-and-smell-the-coffee moments. Shanicka and I had been shopping at the mall, and we were walking to the car. We had parked quite a distance away on the opposite side of the mall, and as we were walking, I found myself feeling light-headed and needing to stop to catch my breath. I stood there gasping for air as if I had just run a marathon. *Okay, Tasha—this is* not *good.*

Growing up, I had always been athletic. Throughout high school, I stayed in shape and remained healthy. Yes, I carried weight, but not everybody's a size two! Anyway, there's a difference between having a little extra weight on you and being unhealthy. By the time I had moved to Atlanta, I was busy doing a lot of work at the church and wasn't paying much attention to my health. That moment at the mall when I had to stop and catch my breath served as a warning sign. I didn't say it out loud, but I knew something had to change, and I had to do it quickly!

This was my giant knocking at the door—a battle I had to face.

I had gone through life with lots of self-confidence and was all about celebrating who I was. I boldly declared that big girls rock! I am 100 percent in support of having self-confidence, but not to the point of denying that I am living an unhealthy lifestyle. I had reached a point where my weight could be very detrimental to my health and even my life, so I needed to be completely honest with myself (something that's easier said than done!).

Tasha, you haven't exercised for over a year. You know what you're eating, and you know that you keep gaining weight. Girl, this isn't a good thing. You're literally having to stop to catch your breath.

I knew I had to make an aggressive, conscious decision to live at my best. But those decisions are so hard to make, right? They're difficult to sometimes even talk about. But after years of dieting and working out and trying different things, I realized that I needed an assistant. I needed something to help me. Losing weight was not something I would be able to pull off on my own.

It's a good thing to admit that we need help in certain areas of life. God understands this. After Jesus's death and resurrection, God sent us the Holy Spirit to be our help in living right and as He desires. So, I was resigned to using the template God had established to deal with the battle I was facing—with those thorns in my side. Instead of hoping to find an instant fix, I needed to find formulas to live by.

After praying about my situation and researching different options, I decided the route I could take would be to have weight-loss surgery. This wouldn't be the be-all and end-all to my battle, but I knew it could give me some assistance with maintaining a healthier weight. I found an outstanding doctor in Houston and ended up having a sleeve gastrectomy in 2012. This path included several different classes where I learned how to eat more healthily and make better life choices. In essence, it's a total lifestyle change.

The surgery and weight-maintenance plan might not be right for everybody, but I knew it was the right choice for me. Going in, I knew it wasn't going to be magic. It was going to help me, but I still needed to make—and keep making—wise choices. I still had to choose to eat right and exercise. After the procedure, I immediately began to train, and soon I got as healthy as I had ever been. I had started out at 350 pounds and lost 130 pounds. I was the smallest I had been in my entire adult life! But more important than that, I was the *healthiest* I had been as an adult.

So, I slayed my giant and plucked that thorn out of my flesh forever! (Can you hear my laughter?) Nope, not so fast.

Yes, for three years, I remained very consistent with working out and living a healthy lifestyle. On top of that, we were traveling and I was able to move around without losing my breath. I noticed the difference. But still, every single day, I had to make a conscious decision to stay on track. I had to be intentional about my choices because it's so very easy to get off track. The easiest thing is to pick up a bag of chips or have a piece of cake. And even with good, healthy choices, life happens. Those little nagging bad habits can find a way back into our lives.

About four or five years after the surgery, I found myself making bad eating choices. Life was busy, so it was so easy to make unhealthy choices, especially because I was traveling four to five days a week, living in a different city or state every night. Those Little Debbie snack cakes kept showing up at my doorstep, wondering where I'd been. So the weight started to pick back up. There I went once again with this up-and-down roller coaster. This constant war and endless fight! Isn't it exhausting?

Right before my wedding, I found myself needing to make a choice again. *I gotta lose this weight!* And Kenny, my fiancé, was in the same boat as me. In fact, he had gone through the same surgery as I had, so we became partners in starting to work out and eat healthier. We got back at it, and the weight started falling off once again. I was back down to a very comfortable weight on our wedding day in 2017. But even then, it was like fighting an undefeatable giant.

Does this sound familiar? We all have battles we must face in some capacity. But what do you do after you fall away from those good decisions you've been making? Do you start to beat yourself up? Do you simply give up? Do you find yourself back in a rut and feeling hopeless?

That's just life! Life is full of ups and downs—those mountaintops and valleys. It's so full of different seasons, and there are some seasons when you're able to give more to your battle. In my battle with my weight, I've started to fail time and time again. Does this make me stop trying? No way! Each time, I get back up and do it anyway!

When Kenny and I moved to Greenville and got involved in our church, we found ourselves gaining the weight again. Joi (my personal assistant) and I decided we would embark on the Orangetheory Fitness program. I went hardcore. I love Orangetheory; the community and competitive vibe that it has is right up my alley. The program was everything I needed in order to get my life back together. I probably lost about twenty-five pounds, returning to a weight that was comfortable. Joi and I were back in shape, and life was going well. Nothing was going to stop us unless it was something absolutely cataclysmic.

Cue the pandemic.

So in 2020, when the pandemic hit, I ended up gaining that "Quarantine 15" just like almost everybody else. Even though I tried as hard as I could to maintain things by working out at the house, it was hard. And, yes, the weight came back, and it was probably the most I had gained since 2012.

Do you see this pattern in my life? Can you relate to it? The up and the down, and the down and the up. Sometimes we win, and sometimes we lose.

We can always stand back up after falling. Don't ever beat yourself down so much that you remain on the ground. Don't ever feel like something has defeated you for good. Never! It might just be a thorn that you have to overcome daily. Sometimes it might even be a minute-by-minute choice.

We can choose to make the conscious decision to live at our best, time and time again.

*   *   *

We all want miracles to happen overnight. Everybody wants a miracle—for God to rain down manna from heaven. But most of the time, miracles aren't what's best for us. In the case of my battle with weight, it's obviously been a long war. This battle has taught me so many valuable lessons, including a big one: You have to walk out the process of healing at the pace of God's deliverance. This helps to mature you. Think about it: If we lived one miracle at a time, we would be the most immature, spoiled brats in the world!

I believe that some things—actually, most things—God wants us to learn by principle. That's why He left so many principles in Scripture. He wants us to live by principles because that's what is going to make us wise. If we live based on miracles, our purpose would be contingent on the next miracle. But God's Word is full of principles that lead us to live the abundant life that He desires for us.

The battles we fight, like my battle with weight, are part of a bigger picture. They are avenues that lead us into learning God's principles and discovering how to walk them out each day.

Let me give you another example of how principles helped me fight a battle in my life. Back in 2012, in the midst of the craziness of "Break Every Chain," Shanicka and I were running our operations. This is no exaggeration: We would have around a hundred booking requests coming in every week! People wanted me to perform at their conferences and their shows and their churches. There were orders for my first album and interest hitting us from every angle and source. Nicka and I were handling everything in-house between the two of us. That in itself was a miracle. And on top of this, we were also traveling all the time, sometimes six days a week! We had been working like this for almost a year, and we were both tired out of our minds.

The pace was taking a toll on both of us. Our parents started calling us with concern. "Y'all are both losing weight. You look tired in the face. We think you guys need to take a break."

In my battle with my weight, working so hard was *not* the way to go about losing pounds! I could feel my body shutting down. We were young, but even then, this was our flesh and bones that we had to take care of. We needed rest.

One day while I was in the Walmart parking lot, we had just picked up some basic household goods and were heading to the car when I began to have a sneezing attack, which wasn't anything new. I have horrible allergies (shout-out to the Atlanta pollen!). On that day in the parking lot, I had to stop to sneeze in my hand, over and over again, and on the last sneeze, I felt something spray onto my palm. When I looked down, I noticed it was blood.

Not long after that happened, in the midst of one of the busiest seasons of my life, I started to get hoarse. I was still doing shows, but I didn't have the vocal control that I was used to. So many frightening thoughts invaded my mind about what could be happening.

Although I was afraid of what the diagnosis might be, I chose to go see a throat specialist anyway. I found one of the most sought-after vocal doctors in the world, Dr. Johns, whom I'll never forget. He examined my vocal cords and ended up detecting a huge, nasty polyp on my left vocal cord. Vocal therapy, rather than surgery, was recommended as the route to take, so the medical experts connected me with my angel, Eva. She was my vocal therapist, but truly she was most definitely sent from God. Every day, Eva coached me, first at the doctor's office and then at her home. I went through therapy for two years until I got my voice back.

As I look back on this now, I know that this medical issue was intentional on God's part. He was telling me that I needed to slow down and learn how to take care of my vocal cords. It was important for me to have that experience. My body was teaching me a valuable lesson that didn't feel good, but it was *for* my good.

You're not invincible, my body said. *If you don't take care of yourself, you won't be here to sing "Break Every Chain,"* God told me. At the time when I lost my voice, I felt devastated. *A health crisis in the middle of this amazing and hectic season?*

My battle came to a climax one day while I sat in my car parked in the garage. I sat in solitude. The weight of not being able to use words pressed down on me. I felt muted, gagged, canceled. The Enemy clutched my heart and filled my thoughts with doubt and despair. But then a whisper of hope entered my soul: *I still have my praise*. The reality of this thought felt like inhaling after swimming up from deep waters. I thought of the truth of this. I couldn't sing, and I didn't know when I'd be able to sing again, but I still had my praise!

My praise is not contingent on my vocal ability. I had no vocal ability, but my soul could still cry out. My body might be broken, but my spirit remained buoyant. I didn't have to mouth lyrics for the Lord. All I needed to do was lift them up to Him.

Nothing can take my praise. Nothing can hold me down. Worship had never been about being in front of the public, about having a stage presence, about performing and producing songs. Worship has always been about running to the feet of Jesus again and again.

Satan wants to silence us, but God hears our hearts and receives the lyrics we may struggle to write. We don't need a microphone to magnify Him. *I'll lift my voice and sing. I'll make my praise resound*. I still had faith in God's plans and purposes for my life. For now, my voice had vanished, but I believed.

Gonna hear it again, gonna hear it again.[1]

This praise was gonna live forever!

Thank God my voice eventually returned. Thank God that many have continued to hear it all over the world.

This battle wasn't simply about the polyps and losing my voice. God brought me through this trial in order to teach me valuable lessons. God was teaching me, "Tasha, your vocal technique is horrible, and you're not going to have a voice in twenty years if you keep singing this way and not taking care of your vocal cords!"

This lesson was about me maturing and growing up. It was about learning how to take care of myself.

*　　*　　*

So, how do we win the battles? The first thing I would encourage is to be honest with ourselves. After I had my surgery in 2012, I looked back at pictures of myself and couldn't believe what I saw. I went to different family members and showed them the photographs.

"Look at these!" I'd say. "You guys were just gonna let me die."

Of course, a lot of them felt bad, but they also acknowledged the obvious: "I didn't want to hurt your feelings" or "I didn't know how you would receive it." Ultimately, I was the one who had to face myself and admit the truth.

Tasha, you weren't being honest with yourself.

I spoke about self-worth all the time, and I shared my own self-confidence. I encouraged others to believe in themselves. But even though I had confidence in myself, I needed to be honest about my eating habits. I needed to admit that too much weight on my body could potentially kill me.

Sometimes we live in denial. It's hard to face the truth, but sometimes we have to hit bottom in order to move forward. We love to talk about how we hate people who lie to us, but I think we lie to ourselves more often than anyone else does. We lie and we create this portrait of ourselves, this picture that we want the rest of the world to receive. They see the real portrait, however, even though we might deny it.

Be honest with yourself about those unhealthy things in your life. Unhealthy habits. Unhealthy relationships. Unhealthy addictions. It might be food for you, but it might be a hundred other things. Whatever it is, we have this ability to create narratives to make these unhealthy things seem less urgent to combat. We can convince ourselves that they're not that serious, that they're not priorities to fight.

At the time of writing this, I've approached my current tour in the healthiest way I've ever done. I know better now than to finish a show and then go to a fast-food drive-through. I'm a mother now. I'm over forty years old. I can't lead an active life if my body is deteriorating from high blood pressure, diabetes, or whatever it might be. If I don't make healthy choices, it's going to be impossible for me to raise my son, because I can't run after him if I can't breathe! If I don't make my battle with my weight an urgent matter, then I'll get off track and it will be impossible for me to go out and minister to the masses since I'll be in a sickbed.

Whatever God is calling you to do will require your body. You have to be honest and make a choice to take care of yourself every day. You can't wait for an overnight miracle. I believe this weight war of mine has been about learning how to make better decisions. If fifty pounds fell off me tomorrow, I would begin to expect that sort of miracle every day. But we can't live like that. We need to learn how to get up and do the things it takes to live abundant lives, and that takes *time*! If we expect immediate results, we won't have the wisdom to maintain our growth.

My last bit of encouragement is for you to persevere! We all battle something. Some challenges in life aren't life-threatening. They might simply be threats to your well-being, to your future, to your family. But letting things go, even small things, can lead to dark places.

We all face giants. Sooner or later, you have to be a big girl or boy and fight. In the process, you will discover that you're not really battling a giant; you're battling yourself. God allowed me to deal with this weight struggle in order to perfect some things inside me, like my addictive personality and my struggle to run to things that are unhealthy. I think this struggle with weight helped me to discipline myself in certain areas. So, ultimately, it wasn't so much about the weight as it was about me making better decisions in order to become a better person.

Here's a wild thought: What if the one area that you feel is a thorn in your side is really there in order to keep you aligned with God's will? That thorn is there to remind you that without God and His strength, you won't ever be able to do anything. That thorn keeps you praying. Your thorn keeps you dependent on God's sovereignty and His strength, not yours. That thorn helps you be a better person and realize that you are flesh and blood, that you're flawed.

DO IT ANYWAY

What are those thorns that you have in your side? How are you confronting them? Are you being honest with yourself about them? When we recognize those giants in our lives and persevere to deal with them every day, we begin to see change in our lives. I encourage you to spend some time journaling and getting super honest with yourself. Making a conscious choice to be a better person doesn't have to be drastic and monumental. It can be something as simple as committing to an account-ability partner. Decide to make a change today. Even if today looks too busy and too daunting, do it anyway!

8

IN LOVE

Sometimes in the storms of life, God brings you peace in the most unexpected places. In 2009, in the midst of battling trust issues and depression, I encountered a calmness that changed my life.

This peace and calmness is named Kenneth Leonard, Jr.

After dealing with a vocal scare for the first time, I had been on voice rest for a month. I still worked, but I wasn't talking, and I definitely wasn't singing. When Bishop Murphy attended a worship conference to teach and sing, I accompanied him to assist however I could. At one point, he sent me to oversee his rehearsal while he was teaching a class, so I went to where the band and singers were practicing. As I entered the room and heard the choir singing "Praise Is What I Do," I instantly knew they were rehearsing the wrong arrangement. I had to fix this quickly.

"Hold on! Who's in charge here? This is the wrong song!"

This was the first time I had spoken in *months*, so maybe I was a little too animated and energetic with my words. A tall, handsome man stood from the keyboard and gently intro-duced himself.

"Hi, my name is Kenneth Leonard," he said. "I'm the music director, and I'll fix whatever you need before the per-formance tonight."

He spoke in a calm way. In fact, it was way *too* calm for me! I thought, *Listen, if I'm worked up,* you *need to be worked up. Why are you so calm?*

As it turns out, Kenneth Leonard is *always* calm. "If there's any changes that need to be made, we can make them," he said.

Kenny (as everybody calls him) was calm, cool, and col-lected. He helped to alleviate the tension and solve any issues before our performance that night. This man was a contrast to my anxiety. His presence immediately shifted the mood in any room.

The next morning, I got up to sing for the first time in quite a while. I sang "Chasing After You," an upbeat and fast song with a lot of energy. The room felt electric, and right away everyone was going bananas. People were laid out on the altar! The worship and praise was intense. It was one of those moments early on in my ministry when people were surprised—no, make that stunned—by the power of the Holy Spirit. They couldn't make themselves leave the ses-sion that morning; they were supposed to go to class, but they just kept praising! Kenny was leading this moment along with me on the keyboard. He told me later he was thinking, *Who is this girl?*

The next day, I received a message from Kenny on Myspace, my social media platform of choice back in 2009.

"Hi, Tasha. This is so not like me at all. I never do this. But I feel like we need to keep in touch."

Our connection was immediately spiritual even though we were moving in two different directions at the time. I shared the feeling that we needed to remain in touch. We stayed friends throughout the years of living in different states and working in different settings. Kenny eventually got married and had children, and for a stint, we lost touch.

One immediate connection Kenny and I shared was our love of music. He grew up loving all kinds of music and dreamed of having a career in it. Even though he lived in the small town of Franklinton, North Carolina, he remained persistent in his calling. As a teenager, he learned on his own how to play and produce music. While attending North Carolina State University to study engineering, he started playing music at a church and became exposed to the world of worship. He saw for the first time that he could indeed have a career in the music business. Playing keys became a passion for him, and opportunities started to roll in.

When I met Kenny, his talents and anointing had allowed him to travel all over the world to places like Africa, Australia, and Europe while on tour with several legendary artists. He understood the music industry and what being a professional musician looked like—both the highs and the lows. He had traveled with many R&B artists as their music director and had produced several records.

Something else Kenny and I had in common was that he experienced his own season of depression and darkness, which took place when his first marriage began to fall apart. He reached out to me while he was going through it, and I was there for him. After all, we had become the best of friends before his marriage, so much that I would sometimes even help him get ready for dates! Then one day, after we had both experienced many dark seasons, the truth dawned on me.

"You have feelings for me," I said to him. Typical Tasha, jumping out there and saying something like that! But it was true.

It would have been easy to ignore the invisible pull we felt as God was bringing us together. Kenny had three incredible children from previous relationships. We could have looked at the facts and said, *Logically, this is too hard. Too complicated. This won't work*. But many things in life are too hard and too complicated to do on our own. That's why we have to stay in tune with God's voice throughout life's noise. We have to pay attention to spiritual guidance instead of taking the path of least resistance. And that's what Kenny and I did.

If you follow where God is leading no matter the direction you *think* you should be going, you will cultivate an ability to withstand the pressure even when things aren't easy. The key is to pay attention to Him. The path He is steering you toward may seem difficult or even impossible, but don't let that be a stumbling block.

Kenny and I persevered as friends through hardships and conflicts. If God is guiding us somewhere, then we have to be patient, knowing He has a greater reward in store for us. For Kenny and me, that reward was a marriage built on a strong foundation.

*   *   *

After two years of much planning and wise counsel, Kenny and I surprised those closest to us with a private wedding ceremony on March 3, 2017. Since Kenny and I both lived very public lives, we wanted the opportunity to celebrate this special event privately with just family and friends. Because both of us come from musical families, we all shared a beautiful worship moment at the wedding where everybody sang "Alpha and Omega." It sounded like a heavenly choir. Having both of our families worshipping together carried such spiritual significance for us.

The biggest blessing from marrying Kenny was that I immediately gained three bonus babies: Alanaa, James (Nehemiah), and Symphony! Along with this blessing came the difficult yet rewarding challenge of blending our family together and creating an atmosphere of love, acceptance, and understanding. I love challenges, and this was one of the biggest ones God had ever given me.

Blending a family requires hard work, but it can be done! We have to be patient. We have to know there are going to be difficult times. We have to accept that we won't just get a free pass initially, that we won't automatically fit seamlessly together. Anytime we enter into a new world, we must get acquainted with the culture and find our place. We have to find a way to enter into this new dynamic and figure out how we all belong, especially when there's already a culture and a family flow in place.

Hear me—the kids aren't going to make it easy. There will be times of manipulation and playing adults against each other. We went through all this. It's a type of safeguard instinct children have that I completely understand now. It's difficult for them to articulate the importance of having a safety net, so they create boundaries that challenge whatever's interrupting their normalcy until they can be sure they're safe.

Perhaps the one who this change affected the most was our oldest daughter, Alanaa. She was fifteen, so she was old enough to understand the transformation that was happening. She held her own views about everything, and her own confusion and frustrations. The pattern of life she had grown accustomed to was now being interrupted.

For our first Christmas together, we took a trip down south to Brunswick, Georgia (Jekyll Island), and visited my mom, who lived about a half hour away. I realized very quickly that being a parent meant figuring out the kids' many different moods, helping them remember the basics daily, and dealing with lots and lots of energy, especially for our youngest, Symphony. She was bouncing off the walls, so I thought I was doing the right thing to monitor her every move and discipline her every time she turned a flip or ran across the room. We quickly found out that I am more of a disciplinarian than Kenny is. He disciplines as well, but I'm the one saying, "Stop doing that! Get down!" right away, while he has more of a soft touch. He's a processor, so his discipline is infused with much thought and information. He's the calm straight shooter.

Anyway, while we were all on vacation, Symphony was jumping around the whole time, and I was calling out every little thing. Alanaa ended up getting a little offended at my reactions, feeling as though I was being too harsh with her baby sister. So upon our returning home for the night, she called Symphony's mom, Shya, and shared her disapproval. Shya immediately called Kenny to discuss the children's concerns.

"Can you talk to Tasha about being a little softer with the kids?" she asked.

I was right next to Kenny when she said this, so I heard every word. I told her, "I can hear you."

We had one of those difficult conversations, and after we finished, Kenny decided to have a heart-to-heart conversation with Alanaa.

"Let's just call the kids in here," Kenny said. "We're going to handle this right now."

It's always easier to wait, to say nothing, to let a day or a week or a month pass before addressing a difficult situation. But the best thing to do is address an issue right away. To communicate about it. That's what our family did: We created a transparent culture we try to maintain even now. After the kids came in, Kenny asked Alanaa to explain how she was feeling, and soon we got into a superheated, supercharged discussion, one of those that can either tear you apart or pull you closer together. Thank God this conversation was one that brought us closer together!

This was a shifting moment for me in our family. Some hard things were said, and I believe that Alanaa and I heard each other. At the end of the day, we were all able to share with each other some feelings that hadn't been shared before.

"I love you guys, and I know my way of parenting may be different than the other parents'," I said to the children. "But if you allow me to try to be a parent and let me work on *me*, we can get through this."

That difficult conversation changed so much, and it easily could not have happened. But since we had that conversation, it led to my learning more about how to better understand the kids' unique personalities and the style of discipline they best respond to. It also led to Alanaa understanding where I was coming from. I was able to tell the kids that I was going to love all of them and that I wasn't just going to be here today and gone tomorrow. That I would love them for the long haul! Alanaa and I have an amazing relationship today. She's my little lady, and that she will forever be!

Did I want to address those heavy issues right away with our children? No way. But in my love for Kenny and the kids, we did it anyway.

* * *

When Kenny and I married, we knew that it would take work to blend and build a strong and loving family, but we were both willing to commit to all that it would take. Blended families require consistent willingness to press in with honesty, listening ears, and intentionality. It's one thing to work on these techniques with the children, but I would also have to work on them with Shya, Kenny's ex-wife and the mother of our two middle children.

Early on, there were some uncomfortable moments with Shya, such as the phone call while we were at Jekyll Island. But I knew that things were shifting with our relationship when she reached out after seeing an interview of actor Will Smith's ex-wife, Sheree Zampino. In the interview, Sheree explained how she had come to develop a trust with Will's wife Jada Pinkett Smith by seeing how much Jada loved

Sheree's child.[1] Shya called me and told me she had just watched this interview.

"The way you love my children makes me love you, too," she told me.

She invited me out to lunch, and ever since then, we've been building a healthy relationship that I believe is an example to so many others. I'm so grateful.

None of this has been easy, yet we've done it anyway. In order to build relationships and create safe and healthy boundaries, we have to take the initial difficult steps of talking things out with honor and respect. We have to be willing to be vulnerable and to even be hurt before being loved. Sometimes that's the only way that a loving and healthy thing can grow.

DO IT ANYWAY

Even if you don't have firsthand experience with blended families, you probably know how family relationships can be challenging and require honesty. How can you be more vulnerable and honest in your closest and most important relationships? Where is God working in your life to cause you to grow and change for the good of your family? During times of tension and turmoil within those relationships, resist the urge to argue and fight, and instead listen. Even when it's difficult to be patient and loving, do it anyway!

9

IN TIMES OF DESPAIR

At many times throughout my life, my faith was tested and my peace troubled on all different fronts—from personal struggles to professional setbacks. Despite the darkness surrounding me, I knew there was a lesson in all this for me.

When the mountaintop seems far away and you forget the joy that made you start climbing in the first place, always remember that God is still with you. You might be in a dark season when your spirit is full of despair—a season that literally has you questioning your faith—where you wait and wonder and get on your knees and pray to God, *Where are You?*

If you are ever in a season like that, know one thing: God is not only still there, but He is waiting for you and has already orchestrated your resurrection! I know this because God lifted me up during my own dark season. He had a grand plan that was meant all for His glory.

*   *   *

A year into our marriage, Kenny and I found out that I had endometriosis. This condition occurs when endometrial tissue begins to grow outside a woman's uterus. Along with causing severe discomfort, endometriosis can make getting pregnant very difficult. Kenny and I didn't give up on our hopes and dreams to have a child together. Instead, we felt led to see a specialist in Houston who helped us. There was a treatment that I could receive consisting of several shots once a month, but there was a catch: The only way I could get these shots was from my doctor in Houston. So Kenny and I began to fly to Houston once a month for me to receive these injections.

After a year of my trying to get pregnant, we decided to go through with in vitro fertilization (IVF). I was still getting my treatments in Houston, as the doctors won't let a woman do IVF without clearing the uterus of the endometriosis. This journey continued for months and months and then turned into years.

When you're someone who has influence and is constantly being watched by people, you don't have a responsibility to inspire just when you're on the mountain; you have to live out your faith in front of the masses even when you're in those valleys. That is what speaks volumes: the times when you don't lose your faith but instead continue preaching and teaching in a transparent way. That is what Kenny and I continued to do. We walked through the process, continuing the mission God had given us, even on disappointing and devastating days.

The truth is that all of us have some kind of influence. We are all watched by others eventually. If you're a parent, you definitely know what I'm talking about! Moms and dads have such a massive responsibility in taking care of their kids through good times and bad times, and the kids are always watching! The same goes for those leading a business or church and for the colleague and team member too—we underestimate the influence of our presence. We all should deal with our personal struggles in a way that is reflective of our trust and faith.

When you're going through times like this, prayer is the first place you must go. Thankfully, we also had people surrounding us with love and covering us in prayer. People kept pushing and telling us that God was still with us and that He hadn't forgotten His promise to us. Whomever you might have in your life who can help you along during difficult times, lean on them and let them walk with you.

While this was happening, God opened up a new door and gave us a new assignment in late 2019. For a while, my agent— Mike Snider, with William Morris Endeavor (WME)—had been working on trying to get me a show at the historic Ryman Auditorium in Nashville. One of the most famous concert halls in the world, this 2,362-seat venue was the former home of the Grand Ole Opry. When Mike and I had a meeting with the Ryman team, a thrilling idea came up.

"Wouldn't it be amazing to have a live recording at the Ryman?" Mike asked.

After we went on a walk-through with their team, everybody grew excited. This would be the first Christian gospel worship album *ever* to be recorded live at the Ryman,[1] so this was history in the making! (Of course, leave it to me to put a wrinkle in the history books!) We locked down all the details and began the marketing and started selling tickets and already had more than a thousand tickets sold . . .

Then the pandemic hit.

As everybody waited and watched, initially thinking Covid-19 was going to blow over, we soon realized that it was going to be staying a little longer than the two weeks everyone had expected. So we decided to push back our recording date. We all were devastated to think this concert might not end up happening. Our label came to us and said they were being forced to cancel events and reimburse people for sold tickets. They wanted to talk to us to hear our thoughts about this album. Did we want to postpone it? Should we wait and see how long the pandemic was going to last? So Kenny and I prayed about it. God quickly gave me an answer.

"Nope! Things might be shut down, but we're going to do it anyway!"

Now we just had to figure out *if* we could do it anyway.

At that time in 2020, each state had different rules for what was being allowed for public events. Tennessee had very strict rules, and at one point, all the restaurants and stores were shut down for a period. We had to wait to find out what rules would be enforced, so I couldn't even say, "Hey, we're still going to do it!" if the state said we could have only two people in the room at a time. Eventually, it was decided that we were able to have twenty-five people in the building at one time. Twenty-five people *total*! Meaning there wouldn't be anybody in the crowd.

When the label called with that news, I told them we would figure it out. I met with my production team via Zoom and explained the situation. "Hey, guys. We're gonna move forward with this recording, so here's the deal: We can only have twenty-five people in the building. Not in the main room, but in the entire Ryman! From lobby to the stage—everywhere."

Nobody blinked. My team is always up for a challenge! They got creative and figured it out. We invited the family band We The Kingdom to come, but since there are five of them, that would take us to thirty people. However, my band didn't need to be playing, so we decided when it was time for We The Kingdom to come out, our band could leave not only the stage but also the building. So, that's the sort of challenge we faced, and we improvised and thought outside the box.

I felt that we had to proceed with this idea regardless of all the obstacles in front of us. In ten years, I wanted to be able to look back at the event and see that the church wasn't silent during the pandemic. We didn't give up. I hoped people would see a decade from now that we had still worshipped through anxiety, fear, and pain. That we still released songs that would lead people through this challenging season.

*   *   *

After my being diagnosed with endometriosis and starting the process of IVF, Kenny and I looked forward with faith that the God who had seen us through so many times before would surely come through again. I had spent hours and hours in the doctor's office getting hormones, shots, and injections, but I had spent more time praying. The doctors had told us we had one healthy embryo.

For months, we had developed this embryo and said prayers and held on to faith. Then three days before our scheduled recording session at the Ryman, we were given the heartbreaking news that we had lost the baby. The IVF didn't work. I was devastated. During the entire ride to the Ryman, I lay in the back of the bus in tears, completely inconsolable. Kenny tried everything to help me. He was so concerned about taking care of me that he wasn't able to deal with his own grief until later.

"I give up," I told Kenny. "I don't want to go. How do I sing about faith when I have none?"

It was one of the lowest moments of our marriage. Kenny assured me it was my own decision if we would go or not. Of course, it would have been much easier to stay home and grieve in privacy. To sulk and question my faith. And I did all that, yet I did it while still working—moving forward with my assignment and walking it out while wading in our loss.

When Kenny and I arrived, the band was having rehearsals for two days. I'm normally super excited about rehearsals leading up to a recording, but this time I simply didn't have the capacity. I feel that whatever happens happens because God wants it to happen! But on the second day, I decided to get up and go for maybe twenty minutes. When I walked in, they were singing the song "You're Gonna Get the Glory." I joined them onstage but couldn't keep my emotions from pouring out. None of my team realized what Kenny and I were going through. They knew we had been trying with IVF, but nobody was aware we had just lost the baby.

Standing on that rehearsal stage—surrounded by a team who loved me, the music still playing in the background—I spoke into the microphone and bared my soul. "This week has probably been the hardest week of my life, and the most challenging week for my faith."

My words came out slowly, carefully, deliberately. "It was so heavy to the point where, probably up until right now, I wasn't sure that I needed to do this. I've seen God do miracles. I've seen Him work miracles in people's lives. But sometimes you can be faced with—with something so difficult that even what you've seen, you question. And that's where I've been this week. So . . ."

I paused for a moment. "I felt like I needed to share this with you guys. That this time I'm not necessarily ministering just to you. To God's people. I have to minister to myself, and I needed y'all to know that."

Then I shared something that I needed to hear more than my team did. "I don't want to just create pretty songs. We're creating the sound that will birth miracles in people's lives. To rejuvenate their faith. To revive their faith. And even if God doesn't do it, it doesn't mean that He can't."

I closed my eyes and began to weep. Soon Kenny came and embraced me. After our powerful worship, our team set down their mics and laid down their instruments to wrap their arms around Kenny and me. Our team prayed for the two of us in a way I have never seen. They were our strength. They just covered us and consoled us and hugged us, all without knowing any details. To me, that is a picture of true ministry.

I'll say it again: Sometimes you don't know you can do what you've been preaching about until you have to actually do it. And sometimes living the life that we're preaching about isn't easy!

*   *   *

As worship leaders, we often say that we have an audience of One. But in my first Ryman appearance, I *literally* had an audience of one since nobody else was in the room! But you know, it was beautiful. It was gloriously different. And it happened when it could have so easily not happened!

Kenny and I had an excuse—a very good excuse. We had just lost our baby three days earlier. People would have understood why we couldn't come to Nashville. But during those days, when I wasn't hearing a lot in that season, I know that I heard God distinctively tell us to go anyway.

When I sang "You're Gonna Get the Glory," I wasn't simply singing lyrics; I was submitting them before the feet of Jesus. My voice lifted up even after almost three years of letdowns and hard work and putting all kinds of stuff in my body. Whenever I watch the video for the album recording, I see myself bloated from all the medicines that were still inside me. I can see the fatigue in my face. And I even still feel remnants of the pain that I felt in my heart. Yes, there was emotional pain, but there were also physical pains in my body the entire night.

During the IVF process, once you stop with the injections, your uterus is so enlarged that the swelling causes a lot of pain in your lower-abdomen area. Underneath my beautiful tailored suit was an elastic bandage there to keep the pressure off to help with the pain. You don't see me doing a lot of movement onstage in the video because I couldn't move! My uterus was trying to settle, so the doctors had told me not to do a lot of movement. But come on—had they *ever* been to a worship experience like this one?

Nobody except God and Kenny knew what I was going through. We performed all the songs nonstop, and it was glorious. We didn't hold anything back even though there was an audience of only One. When you watch the video, you might think we're singing to a Super Bowl crowd. And that's what I wanted it to be. I didn't want it to feel like a performance given during a pandemic. I wanted people to watch it and feel as if they were having this experience at their own church.

During this period of very bad news in our world, people needed good news. They needed the good news of Jesus Christ. On September 25, 2020, I once again had an amazing opportunity to spread the gospel and inspiration to people with the release of my album *Royalty: Live at the Ryman*. What an honor to be called to sing about God and bring glory to Him! It's not about me and Kenny and our team; it's about Someone greater than us!

*   *   *

I believe that every album has its own assignment and that every song I sing has its own purpose. Every one of my albums takes me back to the season I was in when it was created. I minister through personal experiences, so my songs and albums are always extremely transparent. *Royalty: Live* speaks to the season that I was in. And there's one song on the album that was birthed from a lot of pain. Not my own, but my brother's.

Sharé was going through a divorce and having a really difficult time. He was still recovering from our dad's passing. He felt torn between what to do in his ministry and what to do in his life, yet he never gave up. The lyrics were about him. But the magic and the mystery of songs is that they can meet us at whatever crossroads we may find ourselves. For each season of life, certain songs seem to arrive just when we need them, with a word of truth or encouragement for our spirit. Just like "Break Every Chain" met me in my darkness, some songs are meant for specific people at specific times. "Never Gave Up" is one of those:

> *Felt like the walls were closing in*
> *Hard to believe this ain't the end*
> *I was hard-pressed, broken, hopeless*
> *But then*
> *You called me by name*[2]

My songs are like my children: I don't have a favorite; I love them all. Each song has its own personality, its own story, so I never pick favorites. Which one means the most to me shifts during different seasons of my life. But I love all my babies. I love the short ones and the tall ones, the big ones and the small ones.

"Never Gave Up" is especially for those stuck in doubt and fear. That song is a rare find. It's like a jewel that can speak directly to a person who's dealing with anxiety or depression.

In a similar way, *Royalty: Live* is one of those albums. It's not for everybody all at once; it's for those who feel as though their season doesn't look like their assignment. In so many ways, *Royalty* is about staying at the feet of Jesus. In our lives, we go through ups and downs. We might be sitting in the car outside Video Warehouse or standing on the stage before thousands of worshipping women. We might be hiding in our house behind shut blinds, or we might be sharing our story in front of a sea of college students. We might be marrying the love of our life, or we might be struggling to start a family. Through every joy and frustration, the one consistent thing is that God never changes the way He sees us.

He sees His children as royal. And He paid the cost so we could *be* royal! That thought has changed my life forever.

Royalty is aptly titled, because it's reminding us who we are—that we are a holy nation, a royal priesthood, no matter what our situation looks like. This reminder shows us that we *can* rise up and be resurrected from this season we're in! I've learned to celebrate the joys that come and to also embrace the difficulties that arise, because I know the Bible states that "in all things God works for the good of those who love him" (Romans 8:28, NIV).

Sometimes it feels like the walls are closing in. Your doubts are telling you that this is the end. You feel hardpressed and broken and hopeless. But then God calls your name and beckons you to come. He gives you living water. He covers you with love. He reminds you that you are royal.

DO IT ANYWAY

Consider the hard, tough, or tragic experiences you've gone through or are going through. How have you responded? In those not-so-joyful seasons, what lessons are there for you? Imagine how God might move things forward in your life. Remember that even though we give up on ourselves, God doesn't. He can provide the strength we need to carry on and receive the blessings He has in store, which is more than we could imagine. Even when believing in God to redeem your mess feels incredibly challenging, do it anyway.

10

IN THE WAITING

For almost three years, Kenny and I battled infertility. Anyone who has gone through this understands the emotional weight and the pain that come with this journey. There are dark days, moments when we wonder if what we're waiting for is ever going to happen. Times when everything feels so out of our control and hope seems so out of our reach. Times when we wonder if God's promise is ever going to come to pass.

I'm here to tell you that no matter what you're dealing with and no matter what difficult season you might be experiencing, if God promises something to you, it's going to happen. We just gotta have faith and keep believing.

We also have to have patience.

When we receive promises from God, we are inclined to have expectations of *how* God will make those promises come to pass. We formulate ideas on how things are supposed to happen, and we have a tendency to devise a timeline of events in our heads. But sometimes God has other plans. Sometimes He says, "I want to do it this way: My way."

After going through the process of IVF, trying different

ways to have a child, and then eventually losing the baby, nothing seemed to work. Even though our faith had been tested, Kenny and I had not given up; we remained in constant prayer, trusting in God's plan.

One day my husband came to me with an idea. "What about adoption?"

The moment he said it, something inside me instantly agreed. *Maybe this is the path God wants us to take.*

With hearts open to God, we started the journey of adoption, and we quickly realized that it might be as long and arduous a journey as IVF.

I'm not sure what you've heard, but adoption is definitely a kind of labor, and there were plenty of labor pains that accompanied it! Things like paperwork and more paperwork and finding the right agency to use and gathering and sharing information. Perhaps the most challenging labor pains were the unknowns. So, we went through months of that, all while having no idea how long it would take. We knew that the adoption process could be discouraging simply because we didn't know what the outcome looked like. For some people, it takes waiting two, three, or four years before being able to adopt their child. For others, the pain stems from putting all their hope in the promise of receiving a child, only for the birth parents to ultimately change their minds.

Adoption is a huge leap of faith and trust in God.

* * *

Most times when I write a song, it comes from a current personal experience or from an experience that someone I love is going through. In early 2021, about a year into the pandemic, I was asked by NPR to write a song about my life experience during the pandemic or about anything I was feeling. The organization had reached out to different songwriters handpicked to create something about the season we were in. The subject matter could be something we experienced or witnessed personally or where we were emotionally at the time. So I hopped in the car and drove over to a peaceful place to calm myself in order to hear what the song of my heart was for that season.

After I arrived, I began to think about what this song could be about. I wanted it to be very personal, so I began to think of the past year and everything happening in my life. My first thought was about my cousin Sierra.

Early in the pandemic, our family lost Sierra to Covid-19. She lived in New Jersey, a place particularly hard hit. Even at only thirty-one years old, she was one of the ones who didn't make it through. The worst part of her death was that she had to spend her last moments of life alone. Family and friends couldn't be at her side to hold her and console her. Nobody was there to encourage her in any way. So while trying to decide what to write my song about, I couldn't help thinking of my cousin. *What if someone could have been there simply to hold her hand?*

Then I shifted my thoughts and began to think about our adoption journey. *Wouldn't it be great to write a song for this beautiful baby God is going to bring into our lives?*

I thought maybe I could pen a song that would whisper a glimpse of hope during this season where so many could only feel oppressed by the weight of grief. I pulled out my phone and began typing into the notes app:

*I just gotta believe there is goodness around the corner and
    something better is in store for me*[1]

Kenny and I didn't know what was going to happen with our adoption journey. We didn't know if God was even going to bring a child into our lives. As I poured out my heart, I penned lyrics about faith. "There's a reason for all these tears, and there's an answer to these prayers," I wrote in "Gotta Believe."

Kenny and I had come to the place where there was nothing left for us to do except have faith, so I just opened up my heart and shared our story. I wanted to make a declaration with this song:

*It's gonna work out like I knew it would
I'll finish stronger than I thought I could
There's a rainbow behind the clouds
The sun is bursting out
This can't be the end
I know that there is so much more
And I will find an open door
If I only believe*[2]

As I thought about the loss I had experienced and that so many others had experienced, and as I pondered all the decisions Kenny and I were making about moving forward with adoption, I just knew I needed to depend on and lean on my faith. I wanted to tell others—to tell *myself*—that someday we would smile again.

I assumed "Gotta Believe" would be a song that would live on NPR's podcast. Whoever needed to hear it would hear it and hopefully be blessed by it. That was all I thought about the song. I had no idea the label would hear it and be blown away and think it was so great that they'd want to release it as a single. They felt strongly that it would be a blessing to lots of people.

After we released "Gotta Believe" as a single, it didn't take long for it to go to number one on the charts. It also ended up winning a Dove Award. And all along, I sat back in amazement, thinking, *This is just my story. I was just being honest and writing from my heart.*

Sometimes you never know how many people will be blessed by your being open and transparent about your testimony.

*   *   *

Our agent at the Christian adoption agency we chose to work with was an angel! Some nights, she would text Kenny and me to let us know we were on her mind: "I'm thinking about you guys and praying for you! This is going to work. God's hand is in it!"

Little messages like that were the faith nuggets we needed in order to continue to believe and press on. She was there every step of the way. *Every* step. She helped us build our family's profile book, which was a way to give the birth mother an idea of the family her child would be going to. It consisted of photos of our family and summaries of our lives.

After we had completed our profile, it was time for our

faith to go to work. We had done our part, and it was time for God to do His. Our agent was honest with us about any expectations we might have.

"Sometimes these things can take only weeks, but I've seen the process last two years or more," she explained. "But we are people of faith, and we trust God's plans for your family."

That's all we are asked to do: Put in the work, pray, and trust God. I love what it says about this in Deuteronomy 28:1–6:

> If you faithfully obey the voice of the LORD your God, being careful to do all his commandments that I command you today, the LORD your God will set you high above all the nations of the earth. And all these blessings shall come upon you and overtake you, if you obey the voice of the LORD your God. Blessed shall you be in the city, and blessed shall you be in the field. Blessed shall be the fruit of your womb and the fruit of your ground and the fruit of your cattle, the increase of your herds and the young of your flock. Blessed shall be your basket and your kneading bowl. Blessed shall you be when you come in, and blessed shall you be when you go out. (ESV)

This is a promise! No man opens doors, and no man closes them. Doors open when you faithfully obey God. There is no other formula! There is *one* step: Obey God! So don't worry; just wait.

That's what Kenny and I continued to do. We chose five

trusted adoption agencies and sent them our books. Three days later, our agent called us with an exciting and unexpected message.

"Guys, this is rare. It's wild. I've never had something like this happen in all my twenty years of doing this. There's a small agency in Louisiana that has an interesting and rare case. A birth mother just walked into their office expressing her desire to seek adoption for her unborn baby boy. She stated that she felt that God told her this baby needed to go to a well-deserving family. . . . Your profile was listed. . . . We don't know how this happened, because we never sent your profile to this agency!"

I could feel the tingling on my skin as our agent spoke those words.

"There are seven other families whose information has also been sent to the birth mother. She will choose the family she feels is most fitting for the baby."

We spoke to our agent for a few moments, asking her about other details and what we could do to improve our chances of being selected.

She replied, "Kenny, I think it would be a really great idea if you wrote a personal handwritten letter to the mother. I'll make sure she gets it."

Kenny went to his office and began to write a letter sharing our story. He told about our journey through infertility and IVF. He shared that we knew that God was going to send us the promised child and how we had prepared for our child. Then he gave details about us, about our three older children, about how faith grounded our family. He described our story in a heartfelt and humble manner, then ended with telling the mother that we would be honored to have this beautiful baby boy as our son. Kenny took a screenshot of the letter and sent it to our agent.

The next day, our agent called. "She chose you!"

Kenny and I just stared at each other in delightful disbelief. We were completely surprised. We hadn't *dared* to hope that something like this could have happened so quickly. But here's the kicker: The baby boy was due in a month. We had only *four weeks* before our son would enter our lives.

Kenny smiled at me. "We've been pregnant this whole time."

And it was true. Our baby boy was coming home in a month.

Before the baby was born, we had the opportunity to talk to his birth mother twice. We asked her about the things she desired and wanted from us, things about herself. Near the end of the conversation, Kenny told her that he had one question.

"Out of all the people, why did you choose us?"

"I was sitting down reading your letter," the mother said, "and while I was reading it, the baby started kicking."

She paused, her voice sounding emotional. "He chose you. The baby chose you."

I get chills whenever I think about that. Kenny and I held each other and cried. It was a beautiful confirmation of God's love and faithfulness.

*　　*　　*

Waiting for a hope and a dream can seem so long, but you can blink and suddenly everything seems to happen all at once! That's how it felt with our baby boy. We thought that he would arrive after his due date, but he came on the day he was expected. And we thought the labor might go a little longer as well, but no—he wanted into this world! Kenny and I were sitting at our dinner table when a photo came through on our phones with a note of congratulations: Asher Amaris Leonard was waiting to see us!

Asher means "happy/laughter" and Amaris means "chosen by God." We didn't waste any time getting on the road to Louisiana. After a long journey of three years, we would be seeing our son in just *three* days.

We never gave up in those three years. We kept believing in the promise.

It's true—life is full of disappointments, but God "will give you the desires of your heart" if you continue to trust Him (Psalm 37:3–4, ESV). Keep speaking and declaring the promise until you see it. Never let go of your hope in Christ.

Meeting Asher for the first time and watching him be welcomed into our family was beyond what we could have imagined or expected. He is more than what we could have prayed for. He is a reminder of 1 Samuel 1:27: "For this child I prayed, and the LORD has granted me my petition that I made to him" (ESV). For the longest time, Kenny and I would just watch him and wonder, *Is this for real?* Asher lives up to his name. He wakes up laughing. Joy fills the room when he enters!

Asher is a testimony to anyone who may be in a dark season when the promise doesn't look like it will come to pass. I am a living witness that God is going to do exactly what He says in his time.

If you have faith for something and believe it's going to

happen, don't ever give up on it. It can be hard to walk in faith, but keep walking anyway! You might discover that you're closer than you think. I challenge you to remember that there's a rainbow behind the clouds. Picture the sun bursting out!

Believe in God's goodness, and He will surprise you with so much more than you can ever imagine.

DO IT ANYWAY

What song can you sing as you wait for your promise to be fulfilled? What lyric is rising up in your spirit? When I wrote "Gotta Believe," it was a declaration that the promise would come. That our day would arrive. That song will forever be Asher's song, written to him before we ever knew his name.

Think of a time when you remained steadfast through a tough season, and ask yourself how it turned out. Think on the promises that God has already fulfilled in your life. His history of victory is all the hope we need! When we take time to remember all that He has done in our lives and the lives of others, it gives us strength to continue, even when things look hopeless. Press on and do it anyway.

11

IN UNFULFILLED DREAMS

When I was ten years old, I saw a TV commercial for Clark College, now Clark Atlanta University, and became captivated. There were students who looked like me talking about the joys of learning while walking around an HBCU (historically black college or university) campus that looked beautiful. I immediately went to my parents to tell them my goal.

"That's the school I'm gonna go to!"

This dream of mine remained throughout my teenage years. It was the only school I applied to, so after graduating from high school, I began to attend classes at the university. Now, anyone who knows me will tell you that I am the ultimate overachiever, but there was something about completing my degree that frightened me. As the school year began, something wasn't right. Something didn't fit. To be frank, I simply wasn't ready! It was premature for me. Academically, I was ready. But there's so much more than that when you go off to college. I wasn't ready socially. Deep down, there was a tugging for me to go back to Jesup. I felt that I needed a little bit more time at home.

I attended Clark Atlanta University for a year and made some lifelong friends and had interesting experiences but then transferred to Albany State University in Georgia, thinking that maybe changing schools would be the fix. It wasn't! School had never been a place of struggle for me academically, but for some reason, college made me face my greatest fear—failure—and it was crippling. Failure was not a common thing for me. But in college, I was failing badly, and I didn't like it.

On top of that, I continued to feel like I needed to be home and help in ministry. There were so many things that I had learned and seen and gleaned during my time away, so I really believed that I could help push our church to the next level. I decided to share this with my parents and talk it out with them. Education is big in our family, so I wasn't sure what their response would be.

"Dad, I think I need to come home and help out in ministry," I said. "I feel like I can help in the youth ministry, and I can help in music ministry."

My heart's desire was to come alongside them in building our family ministry and to help the community. My parents both agreed with me, so after one semester at Albany State University, I left school and returned home to assist my parents in ministry. I thought I would never look back. Once I was settled into our church again, I submerged myself deeply in the work of ministry and fell in love with it! But as I did, there was a feeling deep inside me that I couldn't shake.

I had left things with my college career unresolved. And somewhere in my heart, I could hear the echoes of that ten-year-old girl saying she was going to graduate from Clark. What happened to her goals and dreams?

Over the years, I tried to bury any thought of continuing my education. I had failed and didn't want to face that again. The place of fear still had a hold on me.

There are places of fear in our lives that make us feel so insecure, so doubtful, and so ashamed that we will do almost anything not to go there. But that is exactly the place I will tell you to go. And I'm telling you because I had to tell myself to go there as well!

*   *   *

I went back home and got involved in ministry at my father's church. This was when I also went back to work at Video Warehouse. But me being me, I had to pursue other ideas and avenues. At one point, I enrolled in a cosmetology school at a local college, but after two weeks, I quit. Not because I was overwhelmed, but because I already knew what they were teaching me! Then I changed my major again, this time to something more ambitious.

I'm going to try criminal justice.

Now, picture the scene. Here I am, busy with leading a thriving youth ministry at church and working at Video Warehouse, all while continuing to sing and perform at different churches, and I suddenly decide I want to get involved in the world of the police, the courts, and corrections! A voice deep down tried to reason with me.

Tasha, this is so far-fetched, girl! What are you thinking?

But I honestly felt as though maybe there was an opportunity to serve in some part of the justice system. So I went to school for just over a semester until one class changed everything. We watched a documentary on Alcatraz, the most infamous prison in the world, located on a small island in San Francisco Bay. From 1934 to 1963, Alcatraz housed some of the most notorious prisoners of its day, and it was virtually impossible to escape from due to the treacherous waters around it. It was a brutal and inhumane penitentiary. By the time the documentary described two guards at Alcatraz getting killed while many others became injured during an attempted prison break, I decided this world was *definitely* not for me! I withdrew from that program immediately after watching that video and never looked back.

Now, let's pause for a minute. Showing that video was probably the *worst* thing that professor could have ever done. *You just lost a student today!* I was out of there. This was just not gonna work out. Ministry was, and still is, more my thing.

I was the same Tasha then that I am now. I've always needed to be doing a lot. Back then, I was still searching for the path to my purpose and seeking God's will for my life. There was no need for me to go into criminal justice, but it was something to do.

Sometimes it's okay to test out different things and decide they're not for us. It's also okay to stop doing something or drop out of something when we figure out it's not aligned with our purpose. That's how we learn and grow. That's how we learn what our true mission in life happens to be.

When I became the youth pastor at Jesup New Life Ministries, we had about twelve students. I started a program on Monday evenings where the children would come to the church to have fun and grow spiritually. They started inviting their friends, and soon the program exploded with hundreds of kids coming. All these kids from everywhere in the community showed up.

Not long after that, my dad talked to me about leading the music on Sunday mornings. This was my opportunity to introduce a praise-and-worship ministry to our church. When I first explained to him what I had in mind, he was a bit hesitant.

"Y'all are going to get up and sing songs that you've practiced?" my dad asked.

"Trust me, Daddy. This is going to work."

That was something I found myself saying to my father over the years. He trusted me. And the worship team launched and was very impactful. Soon this trust and teamwork between the two of us led to my dad and me going to the leadership conference in 2005 and me eventually moving to Atlanta in 2006.

Throughout all this, there was still one void to fill: I hadn't finished college. And the Enemy sure wanted to fill me with doubts about this. Failure has always been a hard place for me, so in the back of my mind, despite all the opportunities that surrounded me, I couldn't help thinking about what I was leaving behind.

You're overachieving in all these areas, but you failed when it came to school, I told myself. These thoughts followed me around the world, trying to taunt and trouble me. This was another form of self-rejection, an area I struggled with for so many years. Can you relate? Do you have some nagging, nasty place of defeat that keeps nipping at your heels no matter how far you walk or run away? Failure was one of mine.

And every time I thought about going back to school, the voice just got louder: *Even if you go back, it's not going to work out. You're going to fail and drop out again. You're a college dropout no matter how successful you are at what you do!* There are times when God gives us a vision. In Habakkuk 2:2, we are told what to do with this:

> GOD answered: "Write this.
>> Write what you see.
> Write it out in big block letters
>> so that it can be read on the run."

When you write the vision on your heart, you won't forget it. It won't let you forget it, even if it has to wait for a long time.

The devil, however, seeks any way to deride your destiny. But when the doubts come, go back to Habakkuk and read on:

> This vision-message is a witness
>> pointing to what's coming.
> It aches for the coming—it can hardly wait!
>> And it doesn't lie.
> If it seems slow in coming, wait.
>> It's on its way. It will come right on time. (verse 3)

That dream and that vision—it's coming. Though it seems slow, it's on its way. We have to be patient and wait and watch for it. It's on its way, and it is going to arrive at the perfect time!

*   *   *

Speaking of arriving at the perfect time, let's fast-forward again to 2017. When I met and married the right man—Kenneth Leonard, Jr.—I entered into a covenant with a spouse who not only encouraged me to overcome my fears but also faced them with me!

While we were living in Greensboro, Kenny and I had a conversation about God calling us to start a ministry. As someone who had never preached before, Kenny felt like he needed to go back to college to learn how to write sermons, teach lessons, and properly dissect Scripture, so he enrolled himself in Valor Christian College and demonstrated commitment, patience, and determination. He spoke to me about his classes with excitement, telling me about the things he was learning and the revelations God had been sharing with him. I couldn't help but become excited myself. In fact, I wanted to attend the same classes. It was my father's personality coming out in me. I was having fun helping Kenny write sermons and papers. I loved everything about what he was doing in school. I would think, *Wow, this class is amazing!*

One day I had a funny thought I shared with Kenny. "Are you trying to trick me into going back to school?" I asked him with a smile.

His leadership was so enticing that it compelled me to try again, to shut down the doubts and do it anyway! I decided I would enroll for a semester. By the time I was taking classes,

Kenny had gone back to North Carolina State to complete his engineering degree, so that's why I loved to tease him about him transferring from the Bible college shortly after I started going there. "You did that just to get me back in school!" I'd tell him.

Was it perfect timing? Definitely not! I was traveling the world doing ministry, cultivating a brand-new marriage, and merging a blended family. But all the professors were super supportive, and I was working hard and loving school! In the back of my mind, the doubts began to dissipate and a louder voice began to shout, *I can do this!*

For two years, I went to school for pastoral leadership at Valor. In 2020, I received my diploma with an associate's degree in pastoral leadership. And I finished during a pandemic! Take that, doubting Thomases!

After that, I didn't want to stop. I decided to go back to Clark Atlanta during the pandemic because they were offering online courses, something they hadn't offered before. I reached out to their theology department and enrolled there to complete my bachelor's degree. I finished my first semester with all A's!

Once the pandemic was over and the school stopped their virtual classes, I would have to drive to Atlanta for school every week. I was living in Greenville, South Carolina, which was two hours away. I realized quickly that I just didn't have the capacity for that. Right now I'm in the midst of trying to figure out how I can complete the program. (I'll update you in my next book.)

I'm determined to accomplish what my ten-year-old self dreamed! Always remember that it's not too late!

*   *   *

One of the most powerful things we can do for ourselves is overcome the greatest fear in our lives. I've done that before but then discovered that I have another fear to overcome. And then another! Those fears love to fester, don't they?

"Where fear is great, our God is greater."[1]

I love singing about the struggles I have, because in speaking my truth, others are encouraged to realize theirs and overcome them through the power of Jesus Christ.

I love declaring, "Lies of fear, you're not welcome here."[2]

I love revealing, "I'm no longer a slave to fear, for I am a child of God."[3]

I love announcing, "If it's fear that's keeping you from trusting, pour it out, pour it out."[4]

You can't run from your fears; instead, you have to go to the place where the fear dwells and force it to leave.

Sometimes we're not ready for the promise just yet. Sometimes God has other plans for us—plans we can't comprehend, plans that don't always make sense. When something doesn't work out, that doesn't mean you failed. Maybe it isn't your due season just yet. Maybe there's more pruning for you. Maybe God is going to use the season you're facing to grow you more.

Psalm 138:8 says, "Finish what you started in me, GOD. Your love is eternal—don't quit on me now." God is always perfecting the things that concern us. Everything He has called us to, He has equipped us for, and He's setting everything in order.

I didn't get my pastoral degree just for the title or for being able to say I finished it; it's something that is beneficial to my purpose in life. It's something that I can utilize as a pastor and in building our church. It's knowledge that helps Kenny and me in ministry. It's another tool in our hands.

Never flee from your fears. Turn to them. Always be willing to remember your ten-year-old self, to recall your childhood dreams. Be open to continuing to learn and grow. And never, ever consider yourself finished. I'm not finished—not even a little bit!

DO IT ANYWAY

What is the source of your greatest fear, insecurity, or regret? Usually behind that is a deep desire to accomplish something that you surrendered too soon.

You can address your fears and regrets by first going to God in a place of humility. Believe that He can turn grief and sadness into joy and peace! When you triumph over the fear of failure and the regrets of yesterday, you break a stronghold on you and take back your power to shape the story your life tells. Even when you don't have the words to put on the page yet, keep at it and do it anyway!

12

IN YOUR PURPOSE

God has a way of taking our preconceived plans and turning them on their heads. It's amazing sometimes that when we want something—or *don't* want something—He gives us just the opposite! Like when I told Him I didn't want to marry a pastor.

Growing up with a father who was a pastor, I spent my entire life walking with preachers and teachers in ministry. Most of my time existed in the comfort of a church, amid the pews and the altar. So as I became an adult, there was a very specific request that I asked of God when it came to the man I would marry. I prayed, *Lord, I've done the pastor thing my whole life, so can You give me something new?*

You can then imagine my response when, about a year into our marriage, Kenny told me he felt the calling to go into ministry as a lead pastor.

"I'm really feeling a call," he said.

"Absolutely not!" I said. "That is *not* okay!"

I jokingly tell everybody that Kenny fooled me, that he kept this one thing from me until after we were married. But, really, it made perfect sense that Kenny felt that calling. Like me, he is the adult child of ministers and leaders and grew up in the church. Despite my initial resistance, I knew we *both* had a calling and a desire to serve God through the assignment of pastoring.

During one Christmas season, Kenny and I were celebrating at a party with John Gray, who was an associate pastor at Lakewood Church in Houston at the time. During a very intimate conversation, John and his wife, Aventer, asked Kenny and me if we would be interested in helping them launch a new church. During that conversation, we had a chance to share with them that we also had a calling to start a ministry maybe three years down the road. For some time, we prayed about the conversation and their offer and felt God's approval. John called some months later and said they would be taking over a ministry in Greenville, South Carolina. He wanted us to come alongside them and be the lead worship pastors. This assignment was new and fresh for us. Even though I had been a worship pastor before, this would be our first time leading in this capacity as a couple. Kenny had been the music director for several legendary artists and been the lead instrumentalist at his home church for many years, but now he would be stepping into a pastoral role.

God is always so intentional. Serving the people of Relentless Church will forever be one of our greatest joys. He placed us in a position to serve a group of people who were patient with us, loved us, and allowed us to have flaws and make mistakes to learn from. We are so grateful for the amazing team of people we had the opportunity to grow with during that season. It prepared us for where God was sending us.

That period of time is a reminder to me that there is a valuable lesson in every season. Don't ever forfeit the value of a season by being focused on distractions. Sometimes pain, frustration, worry, heartbreak, or any other measure of discomfort can be sent by the enemy to distract you from the lesson.

We accepted the assignment in 2018, and because this would be the first time we'd serve in pastoral positions together, it was so key for Kenny and me to learn how to cultivate our styles and see how ministry worked for us as a pair. More than anything, we would see a magnificent example of godly collaboration. Not just between the two of us, but within a big group of wonderful and diverse people.

*   *   *

Relentless Church began when the pastor of Redemption Church in Greenville, Apostle Ron Carpenter, announced he was moving his ministry to California. The transition from Redemption Church to Relentless Church began when Pastor John Gray arrived. With this amount of transition, we knew we had to enter into it with much prayer. Whenever there is a lot of change in a church or organization, it's inevitable that some people will experience hurt and emotional warfare. It is human nature to resist change. When we ended up arriving at Relentless Church, there were seventeen new leaders arriving in different roles, so we had to take my dad's advice and truly stay at the feet of Jesus.

For a congregation of ten to fifteen thousand people, there was a lot of emotion about having a whole new leadership team. People who had grown up going to church—friends and pastors—were feeling led to move away or find other places to worship, so there was true grief in the congregation. We didn't want to offend anyone or take for granted the fact that the churchgoers had gone through a lot of change. There had been a major shift in leadership, and now the church members were left with the task of adapting to a new culture and new people. The pain was visible in these men and women.

For me, there was an added element in the fact that they knew me from afar as a "famous" artist, not as a pastor. "She's all over the world! Does she even have time for us?" or "I'm on the fence about her—she just did a song with Nicki Minaj." I could understand that people wondered what I was really all about. None of them knew that my first love was pastoring, that I love the local church and adore God's people. But very quickly, they saw that Kenny and I were committed to building personal relationships with each of them. Just like my father had taught me, the thing that mattered most were the personal lives and souls of God's people. We hosted one-on-one meetings to get to know our team members personally and see how they were feeling about the transition. We wanted them to be open about their expectations from us as their worship leaders.

There was a lot of media attention regarding the church transition. John Gray was a big personality and well known as a major voice and leader in the church. The media really loved playing off of all that. (They were calling us the Avengers of Worship.) So, of course, there was all this buildup, and people were very verbal about their expectations, both positive and negative. *What's this fame thing all about?* some were asking themselves. But the attention was not our focus. We came in and loved on God's amazing people. It all developed into a beautiful season and experience.

When Kenny and I started as the lead worship pastors, there were four other worship pastors whom we had the incredible opportunity to serve alongside. At the time, this was unheard of, as most churches had only one worship leader and one worship team. All of us entered into this wondering how this would work—or, rather, *if* this would work! There were so many personalities and so many people with their own opinions and experiences! But we all became the closest of friends. Looking back, we can see that God pulled together the perfect group of people for that season of ministry. All of us jelled. Everybody knew their lanes and strengths, and we were all honest about our weaknesses. We celebrated and honored one another with intention and purity!

There was something really remarkable about our team. Among the six of us, there were white pastors and black pastors, male pastors and female pastors. We learned to collaborate and bring our experiences together to create an experience that was so refreshing to the church. It felt like the dReam Center once again, where we wanted to create an experience that was refreshing for everybody. Now you see more churches that have two or three worship pastors, but it wasn't popular before Pastor John introduced this model of leadership.

Pastors would send their leaders to shadow us for a few days. They would ask, "What's your format?" and "What's your formula?" They would tell us they wanted their church to hire two more worship pastors and wanted to know how we handled the process. We would take our documents and plans and send them out to churches, explaining how everything worked. Here's the kicker: There was no initial template for this vision God had given Pastor John. We had never seen it done before. Each of us had to trust God to give us instruction every step of the way.

There won't always be an instruction manual for what God tells you to do. The first step is to get up and move toward where He's directing you!

That time of developing a new program and team opened my eyes to a revelation: Worship pastors have been trying to perform a complicated job alone for years, and a hard realization is that some don't have the grace for certain responsibilities that come with the title. Some don't have the skills to be an administrator, so the challenge for them is to find another person to carry that portion of the assignment.

Collaboration has always been God's idea. We were not created to live without one another. I think that's why our cultures worship differently. We have different expressions. In the black community, we have perfected praise, rejoicing, and thanksgiving, while there's a depth of worship in the white community that is also necessary in our walk with Christ. Bishop Murphy would express that God's heart concerning this is, I created you different so you can never live without one another (see Romans 12:4–5).

There's something I can learn from contemporary Christian music (CCM) artists, and there's so much they can learn from me. And I think God made us that way on purpose. My hope and prayer is that one day there will be no division. No separation between CCM and gospel. We are all carrying the gospel on the wings of a melody!

*   *   *

To be called a worship leader, I have to be able to lead those in the pews somewhere that I've already been. So if I've never experienced or encountered Jesus in my personal time, I can't take anyone there. The main key is getting to know Him for myself.

When we first began to rehearse with our team at Relentless, I went in with a worship-first mindset. This was big for us. Like any large gathering I've been part of, the first thing I wanted to do was worship together.

"Guys, this is what's important," I explained to our team. "This is what's going to help us build together. Let's go to the feet of Jesus."

All they knew coming into that first rehearsal was that I was Tasha Cobbs Leonard. But I showed up first as a pastor, one who really cares. I think they could see that I knew that the spiritual lives of our worship team needed to be nourished before we could minister to other lives.

The key is having a personal relationship with Jesus Christ. The way I worship on the stage is just a glimpse into the way I worship in my home. When I'm preparing for my day, I turn on my Bible app and just let the audio play. I play worship music throughout our home to set an atmosphere. Sometimes I just talk with God, both out loud and in my head. But I believe you have to have a relationship with Him in order to make an impact spiritually on somebody else.

I think we've all been there where you can get so caught up in life that worship can become an afterthought. Whether you're leading worship, a business meeting, or a dance party for your kids, you have to be intentional about making sure you're spending quality time with God and His Word. There were moments early in my ministry, when I was leading worship at the dReam Center, when I got entangled in the routine: *Show up, sing your three songs, then sit down.* But I think the blessing of maturity is that there comes a point when you know what's important. I've figured out that I need to set aside time to meet with God every day, sometimes several times a day.

It's a growing process for us all, regardless of what jobs we have. When I see young worship leaders not making being with God a priority, I pray that they come out of whatever season they're in. But we all have those periods in our lives where it's too easy not to spend time with God and in His Word. The good thing is that our God is so gracious. He's so loving and kind and so patient. He's going to walk with us through every season.

*   *   *

Leading at Relentless Church wasn't always easy. Some of the people were broken and had walls built around them that were difficult to break. But God planted us with this body of people on purpose. We demonstrated Christ's love to them and allowed them to be honest with how their hearts felt. We loved them and carried their feelings on our shoulders through our worship. There was an incredible movement of God during the two years we were there, one full of healing and reconciliation.

The calling to become a pastor that Kenny had felt before arriving at Relentless remained there. For those two years, he had been walking with Pastor Dharius Daniels and our spiritual fathers, Bishop William Murphy III and Bishop Bryan J. Pierce, Sr. We were definitely spiritually covered! We had been talking to them about the transition to start a new church, making sure that we did everything in the right order and that we were prepared.

Our team and all the people in our department whom we pastored supported our decision 100 percent. It was definitely hard to leave. We all cried, but everyone said they knew our hearts—that they would think nothing less of us as we pursued God's calling. They supported us. It's not hard to follow God, but it *is* hard to say goodbye! At one of our farewell parties, every single person there had a story to tell about our time at the church. What a blessing! We loved those people and cherished our time with them and still have some of those relationships to this day.

We were so excited and nervous to step into our next season! We had prayed and settled on calling our church the Purpose Place, a name I love dearly. So many of us struggle with our purpose. We ask ourselves what we're supposed to be doing. I believe that every single day, God reveals His wisdom to us and reminds us of our purpose, but we have to go to the feet of Jesus to hear it!

As we were planning for the Purpose Place (while at the same time planning the live album recording at the Ryman Auditorium), Kenny and I were pretty confident that we could figure this thing out. We're church kids, so we know how church goes. We sat down with our pastors and drew up our mission and vision for the church. We had an auditorium already picked out and rented and were ready to start having pop-up services. From traveling the world doing worship, we had all these amazing ideas and expectations. We had a worship-encounter calendar and wanted to train the worship team in the creative arts. I mean, we had it all written down and ready to go!

Bam—then came the pandemic!

Have you ever had a plan that you had spent months or maybe even years preparing for suddenly disappear? That's how it felt to us. Initially, we thought the pandemic would be over after a couple of weeks, but on the third and fourth weeks, we knew that a traditional church was not going to happen.

Okay, God, what do we do now? How do you do church when people can't be in church? And how do you *start* a church when you can't *have* church?

Guess what the Lord told us? *Do it anyway.*

He wanted us to move forward in the plans that we had prepared. But we had no idea what that even looked like! I had to remember all the times when I had been in this sort of situation:

I didn't know how to make an album, but by God's
  grace, I made one anyway!
I didn't know how to mentor and lead others, but by
  God's guidance, I created iLead anyway!
I didn't know if my voice would ever come back, but by
  God's goodness, I worshipped anyway!

One day I was sitting in our family room, when the Lord spoke to me and told me it was time to start a Bible study online. So I went to Kenny and told him this. He smiled and shook his head.

Young Tasha Cobbs

The Cobbs family

Tasha and her cousins

Tasha and Shanicka

Bishop Fritz Cobbs

Tasha and parents, Bertha and Bishop Fritz Cobbs, at the release party for *Grace*.

Tasha with her father, Fritz, and brother, Rosharé

Tasha and her father, Fritz Cobbs

Tasha receives the key to the city of Jesup, Georgia.

Bishop Fritz Cobbs and Bishop
William Murphy

Tasha and Ken Pennell,
former president of
Motown Gospel

Photo by Michael Buckner/Getty Images

Tasha giving her Grammy speech at the 56th
Annual Grammy Awards.

Bishop Fritz Cobbs with
Tasha's Stellar award

Tasha and her mother, Bertha

Tasha and Joel Osteen

Tasha performing with Kierra
Sheard-Kelly

Tasha and Bishop William Murphy

The Athlete's Foot opened fall 2023

Photo by Drea Nicole

Kenneth and Tasha

Photo by Jeremiah Drummond

Photo by Jeremiah Drummond

Asher Leonard

Photo by Jeremiah Drummond

Kenneth, Tasha, and Asher

Photo by Dree Nicole

The Leonard family

"That's just crazy," Kenny said. "God just told me the same thing."

So one month into the pandemic, we had our first Bible study on Zoom. As I said, we were church kids, so we were excited about starting a church and were full of a bunch of ideas. I hadn't been afraid . . . until now. How were we going to start and build a church where you can't touch the people in person, where you can't have a band and singers, where all you have is your kitchen table and computer? This was certainly a new experience—definitely a faith move! We had to trust God fully.

On top of that, Kenny had never given a sermon in his life. He had facilitated workshops before, and he was a master producer and musician, but he had never taught a lesson ever.

So, there we were, launching a new church online. I guess you can say both Kenny and I are the "let's go for it" kind of people! Our love and respect for the beautiful congregants of Relentless Church and our friendship with Pastors John and Aventer was priority and always at the forefront of our thoughts. With that in mind, we chose not to market our Bible studies right away. We believe that proper timing is an act of wisdom. Because of this decision we were able to build the Purpose Place on a solid foundation of love, honor, and respect.

When we began our online services, we didn't know if anyone would show up on our screens, but people did! It was so wildly different from anything we had done before, but it was also quite wonderful. Every week, it was refreshing to watch people logging on to our Zoom meeting without them being forced or pressured to. Nobody was there congratulating them for going to church. People sat in their living rooms crying out before God and taking notes and really growing from the Word being shared through Kenny.

As I said at the start of this chapter, I had once told God I didn't want to marry a pastor. But one of the greatest joys in our marriage has been to watch Kenny pour and pour out and lie at the feet of Jesus as he teaches at our church. I watch him in awe, loving the purity of his heart and his presentation. His lack of experience from the beginning has turned into a blessing. Sometimes when you have traveled the world and been in many churches, you begin to think, *I've got to present and preach in this way.* But Kenny had ministered only with music or behind a keyboard, so it was awesome to watch his creative skills complement his communicative ones as he presented to our church. I'm so proud of that.

Part of the assignment God had given to Kenny and me was to always pour into the community. Community became the foundation of the Purpose Place, and our mission was to restore people's hope. So before we even held our first church service, we did outreach. We visited the hospitals in Spartanburg, South Carolina, and fed the physicians who were serving Covid-19 patients. At our local Target stores, we handed out gift cards to every person who walked through the doors. It wasn't that we were representing the Purpose Place; we were really representing Christ to the people. Even though we didn't have a building and we didn't have a name in the city, there was something very special that God started early on in our ministry.

I have loved serving as the executive pastor of our church,

which has meant I've been able to use all my entrepreneurial administrative gifts. I've been supporting and encouraging Kenny all the way, assisting him however I can as he continues to hone his teaching skills.

We called our services "Purpose Nights" and pre-recorded the services on Monday evenings to be aired the following Sunday morning. One Monday night, people just started showing up, and those people brought their friends and families. Since the auditorium we had first chosen was no longer available due to the pandemic, we had found a small conference room in the Spartanburg Chapman Cultural Center. We were so small that we couldn't use a full band, and some of the band members had to stand outside the room. With only one camera for the stage, we could never get the entire band to fit on the screen. We renamed the services "Monday Night Momentum," and it wasn't long before we outgrew that space and had to find another one. It's been fun to see how we've grown to two services now and more than five hundred members.

This season was so necessary for us because God didn't want us to show up with our "church knowledge"; He wanted to train us how to do something very new. Even our mentors and staff eventually told us that we were groundbreaking with what we were doing, that very few churches were doing what we were doing—starting a church from scratch during a pandemic. God had other plans and a great purpose for us!

*   *   *

Let's go back to those ideas that we might have for our lives, those we have dreamed about and maybe even planned for.

Sometimes our ideas don't come to fruition. But God has a purpose with everything that happens in our lives. Sometimes He gives us something to make us stronger and help us understand our purpose even more.

I believe the pandemic was a reboot for churches. It allowed us to explore what our personal relationship with Jesus Christ looked like outside of having a worship leader urging us to lift up our hands. We learned to lift our hands on our own and pray on our own and study the Bible on our own. For some people, it was a time when their faith grew stronger. For others, as they came back to in-person church, they were looking for a savior to help them manage with the trauma they had gone through. We were ready to serve them.

Whenever we find our plans derailed or our expectations defeated, let's look at Romans 8:18–21:

> I don't think there's any comparison between the present hard times and the coming good times. The created world itself can hardly wait for what's coming next. Everything in creation is being more or less held back. God reins it in until both creation and all the creatures are ready and can be released at the same moment into the glorious times ahead. Meanwhile, the joyful anticipation deepens.

I love what that passage says about going through difficulties. Jesus doesn't want us to be anxious but rather desires for us to wait in anticipation:

> The moment we get tired in the waiting, God's Spirit is right alongside helping us along. If we don't know

how or what to pray, it doesn't matter. He does our praying in and for us, making prayer out of our wordless sighs, our aching groans. He knows us far better than we know ourselves, knows our pregnant condition, and keeps us present before God. That's why we can be so sure that every detail in our lives of love for God is worked into something good. (verses 26–28)

Jesus is praying for us! Can we just pause and try to fathom that? And when we trust that He's doing this, we won't be weary in the waiting, the wondering, and the unknown. Instead, our faith and our spirits will expand!

DO IT ANYWAY

What hopes or dreams in your life haven't gone the way you planned for them to go? Have any expectations or experiences caused you to stall and stop in your walk with God? Take a few minutes to think about how the unexpected turn of events is equipping and preparing you. What does "doing it anyway" look like for you as you boldly walk in faith? Never forget that God knows us far better than we know ourselves and has a good plan waiting for you. Even when pursuing your God-given dream looks preposterous, do it anyway!

IN IMPOSSIBLE VENTURES

When God tells you to do something His way, no other opinion matters. Not even our own. The choice might seem impossible and even illogical. The timing might be impractical. The work might feel insurmountable. But when an instruction comes from God, we should act immediately. We have to know in our hearts that the decision is for our good! We see this level of obedience often through the life of Abram (later given the name *Abraham* by God):

> The LORD had said to Abram, "Go from your country, your people and your father's household to the land I will show you.
>
> "I will make you into a great nation,
>   and I will bless you;
> I will make your name great,
>   and you will be a blessing.
> I will bless those who bless you,
>   and whoever curses you I will curse;

and all peoples on earth
will be blessed through you."

So Abram went, as the LORD had told him. (Genesis 12:1–4, NIV)

On a single word from God, Abram gathered his wife and all his possessions and set out to an unknown destination. What a measure of faith! When was the last time you've heard a word from God and without hesitation, rebuttal, or questioning obeyed immediately?

There have been instances when some of my choices have surprised even me. One great example is when I decided to record my first album. The very idea to make the album was unexpected, but I surprised myself further by figuring out a way to actually do it. The real craziness came when I began to work on my second album, *Grace*. I knew where God wanted me to record the album, so I shared this with the heads of the label company.

"I feel like God is telling me to go to a certain church in Montgomery for my recording."

Right away, I could see that they were confused. "Montgomery?" someone asked. "Montgomery where?"

"Montgomery, Alabama."

There was a momentary pause. "Are you sure you want to go there? We can go to a more visible city like Chicago or Atlanta."

"I have to obey God," I told them. "This live recording has to happen in Montgomery."

There was more to this decision. As I prepared to create my first album with a label, I wanted to make sure there was a purity in the room. That was one of the reasons why I had never wanted to sign with a label in the first place. I always feared that it would tamper with the purity of my worship.

Sometimes when a door opens, you have to make sure that God is the one who opened it. And you have to be careful about where you go once you've stepped through it. Just because there's a door in front of you doesn't necessarily mean it's *your* door. There were several opportunities presented for me to capture my live recordings in more prominent and well-known locations, but those weren't my doors.

For my first release with a label, I was committed to not forgetting why the whole thing was happening. Everything that had led up to that point hadn't been because of our perfect planning; it had been because of God's plans—God's surprises. So the location we needed to find for this recording had to be chosen not for its prominence or its high-end equipment or any reasons other than this: We needed a place where God would meet us. A place where we could capture the freedom of worship, not just a well-polished recording.

I also felt as though the people who attended the recording needed to have sacrificed to be there. I didn't want it to be a quick trip over to the big city to hear a performance. I needed them to be there solely for a worship experience. I didn't want them to say, "I'm going to see Tasha Cobbs"; I wanted them to say, "I'm going to Montgomery, Alabama, to encounter God!"

There was one thing about the church I had chosen: I had never been to it in my life. Ever. I had never seen the inside, so I didn't know what it looked like. I didn't even know if they had sound equipment for the recording! (Do you think I'm crazy now?)

Over the years, I had been invited by Pastor Hart Ramsey to sing at the church he founded, Northview Christian Church, in Dothan, Alabama. It was a beautiful church that I loved to visit—such a refreshing place, like a second church home for me. So you would have thought that God would have led me to choose *this* church, right? But they had another campus that was located in Montgomery. It was fairly new and still being established, but that's the one God instructed me to use. When He gave me a sense of peace—a settling in my spirit—I knew that was the one to go to.

Maybe I just like taking risks. I'm always up for a good challenge when God gives it!

When I called Pastor Ramsey and told him that I felt that God was telling me to go to his church in Montgomery for the recording, his first response was to ask me if I was sure I didn't want to use the Dothan facility. Once he realized I was settled on my decision, he was excited about it and welcomed me there. But he neglected to tell me a certain bit of information at the time. The Montgomery building didn't have much of the audio or visual equipment we needed to capture the experience, so Pastor Ramsey had to quickly get to work on some upgrades and purchases. The week after we spoke, he went and purchased everything necessary and then outfitted the church so we could do the recording there! I still can't believe this.

Not only is it hard to believe that Pastor Ramsey did this, but I still can't believe the label agreed to the plan. Honestly, my label pretty much spoiled me! This never happens for new artists. For most, the label would say, "You're going to a church that has all the proper equipment." But they trusted me. They trusted that God was leading us to the right place. And He did!

On the afternoon of the recording, the parking lot was packed with people waiting. My team came to me, excited to tell me about the situation. They said people were camped out on chairs outside their cars! I was stunned and had to see it for myself. People were actually "tailgating" before the experience! The church was so packed that we literally had to turn people away.

The rest, as we love to say, is history. That recording was so special. It included "Break Every Chain," a song I knew would be a blessing to many, but I had no idea how impactful it would become. I couldn't have imagined all the attention the event would draw. Not because of the singer and not because of the place, but because God had a plan.

When God speaks to us, our one responsibility is to give a simple yes!

Kenny says that he's never met anybody who responds so fast to God's calling. If God tells me to do something, he says, I do it immediately. There have been many times I've been hesitant and sometimes disobedient, but what I've learned is that obedience is much better than sacrifice, as seen in 1 Samuel 15:22:

> Does the LORD delight in burnt offerings and
>   sacrifices
>   as much as in obeying the LORD?

To obey is better than sacrifice,
  and to heed is better than the fat of rams. (NIV)

Yes, God commanded the people to give burnt offerings and sacrifices, but more important than that was obeying Him. Obedience can be scary, but I'm much more afraid to be disobedient. I'd rather obey when I don't understand, and when other people don't understand, than to simply do what looks reasonable and easy.

When I walked into that church in Montgomery for the first time, I thought, *This is perfect!* I knew in my spirit that it would be. But I had no idea that just a few days earlier, it was far from perfect. I didn't know that the pastor had gone out and bought equipment. I didn't know the work that had gone into transforming the church. That's just like God!

We have the tendency to focus on the imperfections, the lack of preparation or proper education, but He's only asking for our yes. We can't see how He's working out the kinks behind the scenes. If you've been hesitant to move forward in what God has instructed you to do, I triple-dare you to get up and start today. The same God who came through for Abram will come through for you. I'm a living witness!

*   *   *

I felt led to lean into another assignment a few years after my father passed away. The idea came not in some spectacular fashion but rather in the way many of my ideas come. I was sitting in my bedroom wondering how I could honor my father. How could I celebrate his life and legacy to remember him in a special way?

Well, you know, our family loves eyewear. And as I pictured my father, I could see the glasses he wore later in life. What about starting an eyewear line in his honor?

How are you gonna do that, girl? The voice of doubt was loud. So I shared the idea with some of my friends. I even knew the name I'd call it: Fritz Eyewear, named after Daddy!

I reached out to a company that was already helping other influencers and people start eyewear brands and explained my intentions. The employees loved the idea and the name and agreed to partner with me to make it happen.

"Justin, I'm working on something big and I need a logo," I said to my longtime friend and designer. "I'm starting an eyewear line."

Ah—my team! They never know what I'm going to throw at them next, but they also never say no. Justin jumped on this assignment immediately and soon sent me back a logo that I loved. It has a signature that looks exactly the way my father would sign his name. It was perfect.

I met again with the eyewear company, and we talked through the process of creating a product line of eyewear and everything that goes into it. There were so many decisions to make. The amount of frames to select were endless, and then there were all the different color choices and materials. I had a lot to educate myself on, but I was fascinated and eager to learn. We worked for a while on building a line I would be proud of, and in 2018, we were ready to launch the Fritz Eyewear Collection with four fabulous frames.

Having a product with my dad's name on it wasn't the only reason this eyewear line made so much sense. As I said in the press release, my father was one of the kindest and most loving people you would ever meet. He was truly a man after God's heart. At the end of each of our worship services, he always instructed the congregation, "Love everybody." Daddy was a living, breathing example of God's love on the earth, so whenever people wore frames from the Fritz Eyewear Collection, I wanted them to be inspired to literally see the world and people the way my father did: through the lens of love! I personally pray over each frame that the customer would experience the love of God.

Before the launch, I had been pumping up the eyewear line on my socials and telling people about it. Many people couldn't believe it. "Tasha, you just go against the grain! This is amazing!" But they were so encouraging. On the launch night, people bombarded the website with love and support.

The following year, I felt that God validated this new endeavor when I attended an eyewear expo in Las Vegas. The eyewear universe was completely new to me, but I saw it as an exciting way to spread the love of Jesus beyond the four walls of the church. The company I worked with secured an expo booth for Fritz Eyewear, and as I walked into the huge arena, I was stunned to see thousands—and I mean thousands—of people in attendance. There were hundreds of booths dedicated to the industry of eyewear. I had no idea how big of an industry eyewear was or how everything worked. Buyers and sellers and designers were all represented, and every day there were performances being held on different stages. There were actual eyewear fashion shows! My mind was blown.

Right as I walked through the open doors and started down the row of booths, a guy at the first exhibit spotted me.

His mouth dropped open as he rushed to greet me. "Oh my God!" he said. "I never in my life thought I would ever meet you!" He explained how much I had inspired him. "I listen to your music every day," he said, and tears fell down his cheeks. Soon he was bawling. And it was a true epiphany for me.

Essentially, what he told me was, "I'm not coming to your church, but I listen to your music." As soon as this man greeted me and told me this, I felt a strong confirmation that I was right where I needed to be. I was indeed aligned with purpose. I realized this entrepreneurial work was a chance to go to people who, for whatever reason, may never go to our churches. That conversation was also a reminder that we have to be honest and admit that there are people who may not feel comfortable or even welcome in a church space. We have to go to them! I thought, *Now, this is apostolic ministry!*

Apostolic ministry can be a scary term for us, but it shouldn't be. This is what the apostles did—they took the name of Jesus to people everywhere.

I had spent my life in the comfort of church and worship spaces. I knew what to do there. But when I went to this eye-wear expo, I wasn't sure exactly what to do. However, this man was a sign and a message. All I had to do was trust that God had sent me there, learn what I needed to learn, and grow where I needed to grow in order to open up the doors for me to be the hands and feet of Jesus. I would represent Him in this new industry and be intentional about how I demonstrated His love toward others, and opportunities would pop up just like this one where I could reach out to the man telling me he never thought he would ever meet me.

Talking with that man from the first booth gave me the confirmation I needed to really dive into this entrepreneur world, so I went in with everything. And as any entrepreneur knows, at the front end, you're taking a big risk. You have to pour so much money and time into the vision way before you have something tangible to offer others. For me, the reward came in suddenly being able to meet with people who I may never have had access to! People who have an opportunity to experience God through me. Not just through my music, but through meeting a living, breathing, speaking human being who had something different to offer them.

This eyewear thing was truly eye-opening for me. (And I mean that in all seriousness!) Walking through the doors at this expo felt providential. I very much believe that living into our purpose happens in phases. I truly felt like I was entering my next phase of purpose on this planet.

*   *   *

My experiences with the eyewear industry only stirred this newfound belief that God could use Kenny and me in new and amazing ways. So I kept looking for more doors to open. Even if it seemed like I had gone through enough doors, I continued to wait to see which others opened.

Songs. Eyewear. What was next?

How about sneakers?

I've already mentioned that I played basketball in high school, but I didn't mention that I broke my left big toe when I was in ninth grade. It never healed properly. Over the years, arthritis set in, and the wear and tear was severe enough to cause bone-on-bone excruciating pain. It was the worst pain ever! On top of this, after years of overcompensation on my right foot, my right big toe eventually suffered the same issues.

I used to love wearing heels. I could wear them when I was young, but the older I got, the worse the arthritis became and I wasn't able to wear them anymore, not even for performances. So I decided I'd make lemonade out of the lemons and build a sneaker collection. Heels are overrated anyway!

The truth is, I've always been a sneakerhead. When an exciting (and daunting) opportunity came up to have a franchise in the sneaker world, I couldn't say no to it! A friend who was in the fashion world called me up one day to share that they were starting a program with the specialty-footwear chain the Athlete's Foot. The program was called StAART, which stood for Strategic African American Retail Track. It was a fabulous program created to increase African American representation and ownership within the sneaker industry.

"I thought about you because you love sneakers so much," my friend told me.

She connected me with the company, and Kenny and I had a great conversation with the representatives to learn more about the program. The Athlete's Foot team was seeking to bring a strong black entrepreneur into their community, and they felt like I was a good fit for the program. How incredible was that? I know Dad was up in heaven grinning down on his entrepreneurial girl! Kenny and I moved ahead with this new venture in our lives.

The most exciting part was that I had an opportunity to be an example black and brown girls needed! I could be someone God could use to let them believe that they can be whatever they wanted to be. Maybe some of them would have a similar experience to when I saw the commercial for Clark College. Maybe some girl would see me and tell her parents, "I'm going to own my own sneaker store one day!"

One thing we didn't know was that I was making history. I became one of the few females ever to own a sneaker store that had partnerships with major brands like Nike, Adidas, Vans, and New Balance. I had never even thought of that. I just jumped in not knowing anything other than being passionate about the business.

But I don't want it to sound so easy. Honestly, this was one of the hardest business ventures I'd ever taken on. Kenny and I had never done retail before, and since it was a franchise, we were coming into it as the new kids on the block. Most people already had their ways of doing things. Although we entered not knowing anything, people treated us as if we should already know all the ins and outs, so most things we had to teach ourselves. But in so many ways, God had been preparing Kenny and me for this over the years. (Don't ever think God isn't preparing you for something bigger and better!)

There were challenges that we never could have foreseen. Our team was stretched out (as they always are!) with all the details. And there have been times when I have told myself we are doing too much. *You have to slow down, Tasha. Everybody's capacities are different. You can't have your team doing everything!* But God has put many exceptional people around me who do have the ability to handle so many responsibilities.

The blessing of franchising the Athlete's Foot, just like with the eyewear business, has been the ability to be in a totally different world, where we're able to represent Christ to people who may never come into our churches. All the people we encounter in the business are people we can influence.

Since this business is a faith walk for us, many people have had an opportunity to see how God has come through for every need. There have been times when we needed to meet a deadline or purchase an enormous amount of product, and God has never failed us! Others have seen this reliance and faith, and they have been witnesses to His blessings. They have watched how we lean solely on His promises.

When you put God at the forefront of your endeavors, He never fails. There are times we fail, but *He* never does. Even if it looks like a failure, God never fails.

* * *

You might hear these stories and think, *I could never do something like that! I can't start a business or go into a new industry! I could never take that big of a leap of faith!*

As much as I love risk, I understand. When I was working at Video Warehouse, nobody could have told me that the lessons I learned from being a store manager would later be put into practice for the sneaker store, the eyewear line, and many of the other endeavors I've pursued. I never could have imagined that! Let's say it again: There is a reason for your season, and right now, you are where you are on purpose. You may be preparing for something beyond your ability to fathom!

I encourage you to start at the feet of Jesus and trust God's plan for your life. Seek out your purpose, because when you do, you'll find your path. Knowing your purpose helps you to avoid engaging in plans that don't lead you toward your ultimate calling.

I see this as comparable to David's story in the Bible. David knew his purpose in life. He knew God meant for him to be the king. But immediately after David was anointed, he was sent back to the shepherd's field with the dung and the animals and the stink and the filth! There were certainly times he might have wondered if he would ever fulfill his calling and purpose. But even those bleak times turned him into the man he became.

My season at the video store played an intricate part in who I am. Without that managerial experience, I don't know that I could be as effective of a manager as I am now. Every season plays a part!

Looking back, I can see that so often I say yes before I can think of a reason to say no. When you trust God and walk by faith, then you will know when to act. So many times, there have been situations where I easily could have said no. I could have said no to

recording at the Ryman: Nobody will be there anyway;
trying to adopt a child: It's going to take too long and
    further extend our heartbreak; and
starting an eyewear business: I don't know anything
    about the industry.

It's always easier to say "Maybe next time" or "Maybe somebody else." I said earlier that when God tells us to do something His way, no other opinion matters, not even our own. And as we follow God's lead, we start to learn we can say, "I can do this!" When it seems impossible, we must remind ourselves that "with God all things are possible" (Matthew 19:26, NIV).

DO IT ANYWAY

Think about the last time you said yes to making a big change or doing something you've never done before. What did you learn about yourself and God? Now think about the last opportunity that you let pass you by. What held you back? Was it convenience, security, or fear of the unknown or what others would think? Make a plan for how you'll respond the next time those worries hold you back. When that next door opens for you and you feel God calling you out into the water, jump out there with Him and do it anyway!

14

IN THE LIMELIGHT

I guess you could say I was a peculiar child. When I was only four or five years old, my grandmother and the mothers of our church had a noonday prayer meeting that I attended faithfully during the summer. I would cry hysterically if I wasn't allowed to attend services, rehearsals, or events being held at the church. I *wanted* to go to noonday prayer, and I'd begin to wail if they wouldn't allow me to. So there I'd be, the only preschooler in the church sitting with the mothers at the meeting.

My favorite place to hang out has always been the church, the house of God. "Much is taught, but most is caught." One of my mentors describes our walk with God that way, and it perfectly sums up my childhood. The foundation of my faith comes from watching my parents as I was growing up. I watched how my father led our church with wisdom and how he birthed leaders. I witnessed both of my parents' work ethics. My mother wasn't just a true worshipper; she also has managed her life and career with integrity and accountability. For so many years, I was just catching it all. And it wasn't so much about what my dad said from the pulpit as it was what he showed me with his life.

When I was ten years old, my uncle from Las Vegas visited us. He and my father were the best of friends—as close as brothers could be. They were almost exactly one year apart in age, with my uncle's birthday being on December 25 and my father's the day after. They were definitely twin spirits. My uncle was a strong intercessor and prayer warrior. When he visited, he stayed upstairs in what we called the "upper room." When we didn't have guests, that room was where Daddy would study, pray, and worship. I'm positive the power of God lived there—literally! The upper room was right above mine. One late night, I heard my uncle walking around, pacing the floors, praying before the Lord. By four in the morning, I was exasperated. *I can't sleep! Will somebody please stop him?* I thought.

The next morning, my mom and dad called me out of my room, so I went to the kitchen, where they and my uncle were. He had asked them if he could share with them and me what God had told him concerning my life.

My uncle turned to me with kind eyes and told us, "We all know that there is a strong calling on Tasha's life. Tasha's anointing is peculiar, and the anointing is attractive. Starting from this day forward, both of you have to commit to protecting her gift and covering her anointing, because there will be people and things that will try to attach themselves to her because the anointing is attractive."

As a ten-year-old, I couldn't completely digest everything he was saying, but I knew there was something very significant happening. That moment really changed my whole perspective about my calling and what God had purposed me to do on the earth.

The biblical meaning for *peculiar* as my uncle used it meant special and precious, something protected and valuable.

My anointing is peculiar, I thought with excitement.

From that young age, the conversation with my uncle would remain in my head and my heart. I began to pray a prayer over myself from that day forward: that God would continue to keep me humble at His feet and never take His anointing away from me. I understood this as much as a ten-year-old could, but that request was the posture of my heart.

The prayer has grown into something totally different now that I have an understanding, a revelation of the grace and anointing that God has entrusted me with. But I find it fascinating that I would pray it every day: "Lord, don't take away Your anointing from me." I believe that prayer kept me aware, reminding me that God had something special for me. That prayer kept my calling before my face, even during times when I didn't want to keep seeing it. It was a nagging in my ear: *You don't want to lose your oil, Tasha. You don't want to lose your grace.*

I give my parents kudos, because even though we kept this word as the cornerstone of our lifestyle, they didn't shelter me. Instead of being legalistic, they simply maintained a stance of being led by God. I was allowed to hang out with my friends and go see movies and be a kid like any other. The fact that I had heard the word of God myself just meant there were things I knew I couldn't do. Of course, I had my faults, but I never forgot, *There's something peculiar about who you are, Tasha.*

I knew that my parents were covering me, but I also needed to make sure that *I* was doing what it took to cover myself as well.

*   *   *

I didn't know how important that prayer I began to pray when I was ten years old would become. It is still a prayer to remind me of what my uncle told us. And it's a request to God to keep my heart in the same place it was then: Humbled. Submitted. Grateful.

Sometimes when there are a lot of eyes on us, and there is a gift God has given us, and we hear lots of applause, we can easily think, *Wow, they're clapping for me! I'm so great!* But that's when it's important to go back to the awareness that we are only vessels. We represent Christ. I find myself praying daily, "Keep me humble, Lord. Never take Your grace away from me."

We all have to go before Him in humility. Everything we do should be done for the glory of God. And the place I've always come from has been from a place of worship. Maybe that is why I hadn't originally planned to sing up in front of people, record an album, sign to a label, go on tour, or become "Tasha Cobbs Leonard the gospel singer"!

Early on in my journey, I struggled with the "fame" aspect of my ministry. Sometimes I tried to deny it, and other times I never even thought anything about it. A funny example of this was a story involving Kenny years before we got married. We had been friends for a while; he was living in another city and we kept in touch, so he knew I was visiting churches and singing. He had heard my album *Smile.* One day before his Sunday morning church service, the band was playing music like they always would while people mingled and laughed and socialized. My song "Smile" was part of the preliminary song list, so they started to play the song, and the entire congregation began singing along! This was before the church service, so there was *no* worship leader. The congregation took the lead and started a full worship experience before the service ever began.

Kenny couldn't believe this. His friend Tasha had "made it." It was surreal to him because I was just Tash to him. He thought, *When did she become* the *Tasha Cobbs?*

He stepped away from the keyboard, pulled out his phone, and called me. "Do you know you're, like, blowing up here? I've never heard our church so loud! They were singing 'Smile' before church even started!"

I found it quite hilarious how blown away Kenny was by people's response to my music. Our friendship has always superseded the artistry of who we are. This was the first time he had to wrap his head around the fact that I was known, something *I* didn't want to face either. In fact, for a while, I wanted to run away from it. It made me so uncomfortable. For years, I was challenged with how to respond to the attention without offending people.

After things became so massive with "Break Every Chain," I had to figure out how to handle this fame thing. I felt uncomfortable whenever people asked for pictures with me or autographs, and in some cases, that might have seemed dismissive to people asking for them. I didn't want them to think that I was rude or not approachable, but I also didn't want to take anything away from God's glory. I didn't want to do anything that was *me*-centered instead of *God*-centered.

We all should strive for excellence in whatever we do. We should want to be the best for God. But I didn't become a worship leader in hopes of being a *famous* worship leader; I became a worship leader because I loved leading God's people into the awareness of His presence. Even as people began to be influenced by these songs, something that was always my goal, I didn't want the focus to be on me. But it was hard not to feel like the focus was on me when it came to posing for pictures and signing autographs and doing meet and greets.

I was praying earnestly about this internal conflict one night, and God gave me an encouraging analogy to help. He reminded me of the purpose of a cup:

> *When you drink out of a cup, you can't get to the substance of the cup without recognizing the vessel. So just make sure that when people see the vessel, it brings the attention back to the substance—to what's inside the vessel!*

I loved that illustration, how you can't get to the orange juice without the cup. After God showed me this, I had some peace about my place. I could accept my position. *It's okay for them to see me as long as when they see me, they see Him, too!*

We don't have to stand on stages and be applauded in order to serve God well. Every believer is a cup. Whether performing before thousands, settling little ones down for naps, or working long hours at our lonely home desks, we're called by God to be humble and faithful vessels for the work

He puts in front of us. From signing autographs to typing out friendly texts, every interaction is an opportunity to show Christ to the world.

The questions to ask yourself are, how full is your cup? If you were to offer your cup to someone else, what substance would they see?

From an early age, I've been prophesied over that God is going to do something great through me. And if no one has told you yet, God is going to do great things through you, too! Every time He makes something happen, regardless of what that might be, I'm always blown away by His grace and His goodness. Our God is amazing. Never forget that our God is a great God.

DO IT ANYWAY

Living as a humble vessel before God ultimately comes down to your priorities in life: What are you living for? *Whom* are you living for? What sort of message do you have to deliver to others?

When you live to please God, nothing is going to stop you from sharing that message with others. Don't ever let humility or pride, nerves or anxiety, busyness or fears prevent you from sharing the power and peace of Jesus Christ. Make a commitment to keeping your heart set on pleasing God alone and—one more time now—do it anyway!

CONCLUSION

I love the story of Jesus visiting Mary and Martha. Jesus stopped by the house of the two sisters in Bethany while traveling with His disciples. Martha opened up their home, hosting Jesus and making Him feel welcome. She busied herself preparing a large meal; Martha knew how important Jesus of Nazareth was! But in a frantic state of work, she noticed her sister was sitting at the feet of Jesus, listening to His every word. Martha couldn't believe it! "Master, don't you care that my sister has abandoned the kitchen to me?" Martha said. "Tell her to lend me a hand" (Luke 10:40).

I can imagine Jesus smiling at Martha, perhaps pausing to let her catch her breath, then giving her gentle encouragement. "The Master said, 'Martha, dear Martha, you're fussing far too much and getting yourself worked up over nothing. One thing only is essential, and Mary has chosen it—it's the main course, and won't be taken from her'" (verses 41–42).

The beautiful and revelatory message of this story isn't simply that we all sometimes need to slow down and be more present. It's more than that. Jesus was telling Martha that the most important thing for her, even more important than service, was true worship and devotion to Him. Of course, serving Christ and others with our work, talents, and creativity is obedience to God, but it's even more important to hold on to the posture of being *with* God.

This story repeats the advice my father told me time and time again: The most important thing we can ever do is sit at the feet of Jesus and worship. Jesus also said as much to the Samaritan woman at the well: "The time is coming—indeed it's here now—when true worshipers will worship the Father in spirit and in truth. The Father is looking for those who will worship him that way. For God is Spirit, so those who worship him must worship in spirit and in truth" (John 4:23–24, NLT).

Looking back at the stories in this book, I have so much gratitude to God for each experience. I have such fondness for the wonderful experience of making *Grace* and my very first album, *Smile*. There was an innocence about them, and sometimes it's an innocence I now miss. When I listen to those two albums, I'm reminded of just how ignorant I was about how the music industry works. All I wanted to do was worship. I hear it in the sound of those albums: "Here's my worship, smile. Here's my life, Lord, smile."[1]

I loved to worship. I still do. Maybe that purity and innocence was contagious. People often tell me that my songs articulate their heart to God. They tell me the lyrics offer the words they had been longing to express.

My desire is that when people see me on the stage, they would see God through me. When they hear "Break Every Chain," I want them to hear His voice through mine!

At ten years old or even twenty years old, I didn't have

such a clear revelation of what it meant to remain at the feet of Jesus. But now that I'm older and life has thrown a few things my way, I understand better. When hard times come and it seems easier to try to handle things on our own, the answer is always found at the feet of Jesus. And we go to His feet in prayer, through reading His Word, and in worship.

This book has been about taking action, about going one step further, about trusting God and taking risks through faith. But always examine the posture of your heart before you make a move.

What does God want from you? He doesn't need your hustle. He doesn't need you chasing spotlight moments. He wants *you*! He wants you sitting at His feet, receiving wisdom, knowledge, and instruction.

Before I make a move in my life, I want to make sure that it's God-approved.

So many times, we can open the doors of our hearts and invite Jesus in. "I want You to be part of my life," we say. But then afterward, our failure is that we don't stay seated at His feet. We feel like we have to keep working, stay in motion, and hustle toward our purpose on our own. But we can't know our purpose or how to show up in the world as a vessel without hearing from Him first. Everything else follows one thing: All the perseverance, the courage, the endurance to press on and do it anyway all flows from time spent before His throne.

I don't ever want to move toward a purpose without a word from Jesus.

I don't want to sing a song.

I don't want to build a business.

I don't want to stand on a platform.

I don't want to preach a sermon.

I don't want to quote Scripture or speak a word to anybody.

I don't want to do anything without having approval and an unction from God telling me, "This is what I need you to do, Tasha."

I believe that Mary had that revelation—that though she could be doing so many worthy things at the time, her heart's cry was to be at His feet.

When we sit at the feet of Jesus, it invokes His presence in our lives. I want to encourage you, especially if you feel stuck or broken or confused. If you can't talk to a mentor, if you can't get in touch with a pastor, and if your friends can't offer the help you need, get yourself into God's presence.

"Stay at the feet of Jesus," Daddy used to say. And I say it to you: Stay at the feet of Jesus.

When the world is hounding you for attention, when your schedule feels too full, even when the voice of God feels quiet to you, do it anyway and sit at the throne of Jesus. He will show you what to do and how to move.

I promise you, He will never fail you.

DISCUSSION QUESTIONS

Chapter 1: In Life-Changing Moments

1. How have you felt a calling on your life? How would you describe your purpose? What's your next move?
2. How have you experienced the fear of failing? How can you put these fears at the feet of Jesus?
3. Name three gifts that God has entrusted you with. If you can't think of three, ask Him to reveal more to you.

Chapter 2: In Preparation

1. Have you ever taken a leap of faith, such as accepting a new job or moving to a new city? How did you rely on your faith in making such a big decision?
2. Consider the season you are in right now. Is it easy to trust God's plan? Can you sense how He is preparing you for what lies ahead?
3. In times of doubt, where can you find a renewed hope in the promises God has over your life? Can you find them in your family and friends? In scriptures? In songs?

Chapter 3: In the Heat of the Moment

1. Do you have the right people in your life? If so, who are they and why are they so right? If you don't have the right people, where might you be able to find them?
2. Psalm 37:4 says, "Take delight in the LORD, and he will give you your heart's desires" (NLT). What is God saying to you through this verse?

Chapter 4: In the Storms

1. How have you seen God intervene when you or someone you know journeyed through a difficult, stormy season?
2. In my moment of desperation, I declared out loud, "I curse the spirit of rejection, and I receive the spirt of adoption." What sort of declaration can you make over your life? What do you need to curse, and what do you need to receive?
3. You are chosen. How have you felt this statement to be true in your life? What are you chosen to do? What are your passions?

Chapter 5: In the Midst of Grief

1. Who has been your greatest example of God's love? Have you ever told them that's what they are?
2. What does staying at the feet of Jesus look like for you?
3. How have you lived out your faith in front of others? Have there been difficult times in your life when you were desperate but knew others were watching? What did you do?

Chapter 6: In Pursuit of Passion

1. How much confidence do you have in the skills and callings God has given you? What's holding you back from more confidence?

2. What resources and opportunities to live into your skills and callings has God already placed in your life? (Mentors, friends, classes, asking for help—there may be more support around you than you realize.)

Chapter 7: In Battling Giants

1. Do you believe it when I say, "We can always stand back up after falling"? How do you beat yourself up when you fall? How can you turn that around and become your own biggest encourager?

2. Some battles may never completely disappear from our lives. Thinking about the long game, how might you fight your giant the next time without losing hope or perseverance?

Chapter 8: In Love

1. Are there things in your life that seem too difficult or complicated? How can you stay focused on what God desires for your life instead of those things that have been designed to distract you?

2. How do you handle family difficulties? How would you like to handle them?

3. What are one or two simple things you can begin to change for the good in your family?

Chapter 9: In Times of Despair

1. How comfortable are you in bringing your mess, doubts, and questions to God? Why are you at that comfort level?
2. What would it mean to you and how would it change your life if you believed deep in your bones that you are God's *royal* child?

Chapter 10: In the Waiting

1. What promises and dreams are you hoping will be fulfilled?
2. "No matter what you're dealing with . . . if God promises something to you, it's going to happen. You just gotta have faith and keep believing." What do you think of that statement?
3. How comfortable are you in being transparent with others about the hard things in your life? How might you lean more on your community?

Chapter 11: In Unfulfilled Dreams

1. What are the unfulfilled promises you once made to yourself? What do you sense God leading you to do with those hopes and plans?
2. How have you dealt with fear? What areas in your life does fear still have a hold on?
3. Psalm 138:8 says, "Finish what you started in me, GOD. Your love is eternal—don't quit on me now." How does that shift the way you think and pray about your future?

Chapter 12: In Your Purpose

1. Does collaborating with others come naturally to you, or do you find it difficult? What do you make of the idea of collaborating with God in the way you live your life?
2. How intentional are you in spending quality time with God and His Word? What sets you up best for regular time in His presence, and what regularly draws you away?
3. Look back over your life. What new ventures were you—knowingly or unknowingly—unprepared for, and how did God come through for you?

Chapter 13: In Impossible Ventures

1. I wrote in the beginning of this chapter, "Just because there's a door in front of you doesn't necessarily mean it's *your* door." When have you walked through a door that wasn't yours? Are there doors open right now that you are considering walking through?
2. When facing a risk, we tend to focus on what we don't have (education, financial support, time) instead of what we already do have (a calling, an idea, enough to make a start). How has this been true for you? How do you see God working behind the scenes in your life today?
3. What opportunities do you have to spread the gospel of Jesus outside the four walls of the church?

Chapter 14: In the Limelight

1. When I began to pray, "Lord, don't take away Your anointing from me" as a ten-year-old, I didn't fully un-

derstand what it meant. I still pray it daily, and I've seen it bear fruit in so many ways. What prayer should you pray over yourself every day?

2. How have you grown in humility through the years? How do you prioritize God's glory above people's praise?

3. How have you been a vessel for God in the people and situations around you? What is one way you can be a better carrier of the presence of God?

ACKNOWLEDGMENTS

Thank you, Ma, for being the perfect example for me. Thank you for showing me how to worship. Thank you for the many sacrifices you've made in order to support my purpose and for demonstrating what it means to persevere as a wife, mother, businesswoman, and believer. Thank you for letting your story inspire me to tell mine.

NOTES

Chapter 1: In Life-Changing Moments

1. "Now Behold the Lamb," track 2 on Kirk Franklin and the Family, *Christmas*, GospoCentric, 1995.
2. Vernessa Mitchell, "This Joy," Universal Music Publishing Group, 1998, www.lyrics.com/lyric/3296316/Vernessa+Mitchell/This+Joy.
3. Les Garrett, "This Is the Day," in Arlo F. Newell and Randall Vader, eds., *Worship the Lord: Hymnal of the Church of God* (Anderson, Ind.: Warner, 1989).
4. J. Wilbur Chapman, "One Day," in *Redemption Hymnal* (Buckingham, UK: Rickfords Hill, 1951; 2006). The rock band Casting Crowns made this song popular with their rendition of it, called "Glorious Day (Living He Loved Me)," track 6 on *Until the Whole World Hears*, Beach Street Records, 2009.

Chapter 2: In Preparation

1. "Created to Worship," track 5 on William Murphy, *All Day*, Epic Records, 2005.
2. "For Your Glory," track 4 on Tasha Cobbs, *Grace (Live)*, Motown Gospel, 2013.
3. "For Your Glory," track 4 on Tasha Cobbs, *Grace (Live)*, Motown Gospel, 2013.

Chapter 4: In the Storms

1. "Break Every Chain," track 7 on Tasha Cobbs, *Grace (Live)*, Motown Gospel, 2013.
2. "Break Every Chain," track 4 on Jesus Culture, *Awakening—Live from Chicago*, Sparrow Records, 2011.

Chapter 5: In the Midst of Grief

1. "Grace," track 5 on Tasha Cobbs, *Grace (Live)*, Motown Gospel, 2013.
2. "Yes Lord, Yes," track 7 on Shirley Caesar, *Live . . . In Chicago*, Word Entertainment, 1988.

Chapter 7: In Battling Giants

1. "Nothing Can Take My Praise" (co-written with Tasha Cobbs), track 9 on William Murphy, *God Chaser*, Verity Records, 2013.

Chapter 8: In Love

1. Sara Donnellan, "Sheree Zampino Says Jada Pinkett Smith Was Always 'Amazing' to Her Son Despite 'Friction' in Their Relationship," Us Weekly, August 10, 2022, www.usmagazine.com/celebrity-news/news/sheree-zampino-opens-up-about-coparenting-with-jada-pinkett-smith.

Chapter 9: In Times of Despair

1. RaVal Davis, "Gospel Singer Tasha Cobbs Leonard on Staying Inspired and Building a Body-Positive Business," Forbes, October 20, 2020, www.forbes.com/sites/ravaldavis/2020/10/20/top-gospel-singer-songwriter-tasha-cobbs-leonard-talks-staying-inspired-amidst-a-pandemic/?sh=302c9fca1c20.
2. "Never Gave Up," track 4 on Tasha Cobbs Leonard, *Royalty: Live at the Ryman*, TeeLee Records, 2020.

Chapter 10: In the Waiting

1. "Gotta Believe," track 16 on Tasha Cobbs Leonard, *10 Years of Tasha,* TeeLee Records, 2023.
2. "Gotta Believe," track 16 on Tasha Cobbs Leonard, *10 Years of Tasha,* TeeLee Records, 2023.

Chapter 11: In Unfulfilled Dreams

1. "The Name of Our God," track 1 on Tasha Cobbs Leonard, *Heart. Passion. Pursuit,* Motown Gospel, 2017.
2. "You Must Break," track 15 on Tasha Cobbs Leonard, *Royalty: Live at the Ryman,* TeeLee Records, 2020.
3. "No Longer Slaves," track 1 on Tasha Cobbs Leonard, *Heart. Passion. Pursuit: Live at Passion City Church,* 2018.
4. "Pour It Out," track 13 on Tasha Cobbs Leonard, *Royalty: Live at the Ryman,* TeeLee Records, 2020.

Conclusion

1. "Smile," track 6 on Tasha Cobbs, *Grace (Live),* Motown Gospel, 2013.

ABOUT THE AUTHOR

Two-time Grammy Award–winning singer and songwriter
TASHA COBBS LEONARD is also a successful entrepreneur and
the owner of several businesses. Though she is a worshipper
first, she has proven she is not afraid to mix musical styles.
In 2020, she launched her own record label, called TeeLee
Records, an imprint of Motown Gospel.

Alongside her husband, Kenneth Leonard, Jr., Tasha serves
as executive pastor at their church plant, the Purpose Place.
Originally from Jesup, Georgia, she now lives in Greenville,
South Carolina, with her husband and children.